Fo

Correct Vision

FOUNDATIONS OF THE SPIRITUAL LIFE: CORRECT VISION

Shine International

Foundations of the Spiritual Life: Correct Vision

First edition May 2026
Published by Shine International
Phoenix, Arizona
Email: shinebooksmedia@gmail.com
Website: www.shineinternational.org

ISBN 978-1-962580-09-0

That the God of our Lord Jesus Christ, the Father of glory, may give to you the spirit of wisdom and revelation in the knowledge of Him, the eyes of your understanding being enlightened; that you may know what is the hope of His calling, what are the riches of the glory of His inheritance in the saints

Ephesians 1:17–18

CONTENTS

INTRODUCTION

In this book, we will highlight some essential foundations of the spiritual life in our walk with Christ. Why is it important to review and highlight these foundations?

The Bible speaks about the believers as a *'spiritual house'* (1 Peter 2:5). Also, in 1 Corinthians 3:9, we read: *'For we are God's fellow workers; you are God's field,* ***you are God's building****'*. Foundations are integral to any building. We cannot build on weak or faulty foundations. If a building has solid foundations, it will be strong and can be built up to have higher storeys, but if the building has weak foundations, it will be weak and may collapse, and will not be able to have higher storeys.

The same applies to our spiritual life. If our spiritual foundations are correct and strong, our inner spiritual building will continue to extend and ascend. Also, if our spiritual life is built and established on correct and solid spiritual foundations, we will be *bearers of life,* able to transfer life and light to others and provide them with landmarks and signposts on the path.

In Jeremiah 31:21, we read: *'Set up signposts, make landmarks; set your heart toward the highway, the way in which you went. Turn back, O virgin of Israel.'* Here, God is speaking to His people, saying to them: 'Why are you stumbling in your walk; are you not able to see the way or the signposts?' If our spiritual life is built on solid foundations, we ourselves become signposts on the road for others—the people whom we serve and minister to, or even those whom we aren't directly connected to.

Therefore, in this book, we will discuss three important foundations:

Part 1: Correct Vision of God
Part 2: Correct Vision of Myself
Part 3: Correct Vision of My Enemy

Part 1

CORRECT VISION OF GOD

Why is it important to have a correct vision of God?

We are created in God's image and are called to be transformed into this image.[1] If our vision of God is incomplete, confused, or distorted, it will affect our spiritual growth and transformation into His image. If His image in our mind is limited, our transformation will also be limited. If we have a correct and rich image of God, our transformation will be genuine and rich. Therefore, a correct vision of God leads to genuine and true transformation into God's image.

One of the foundational aspects of this correct vision is that God is a Trinity: Father, Son, and Holy Spirit. Therefore, we will first highlight the importance of knowing God as a Trinity, and then we will discuss in more detail the correct vision related to each Person/Hypostasis of the Trinity.

---

1 Romans 8:29

THE TRINITY

God Revealed Himself as a Trinity

This truth is of great importance to us because the essential and deep needs of human beings can only be satisfied and filled through the full discovery of God as a Trinity. Each Person of the Trinity fulfils an essential need within man.[2]

We can sum up these needs into three main areas:

- Belonging: This refers to the need to belong and is related to one's relationships with others.
- Worth: This refers to the need to be valued and is also connected to the need of man to have deep peace between himself and others, and between himself and creation. (As the need to be valued and the need to have peace are closely related, as we will explain shortly, they are categorised here as one main need).
- Competency: This refers to one's ability to work and accomplish tasks, and the need to be enabled, meaning to discover one's role or mission in life and be enabled to achieve it.

The lack of fulfilment of any of these needs is reflected in various ways in one's life.

- The lack of fulfilment of one's need to belong causes one to feel rejected, unwanted, and unloved.

If one grows up in a family where his parents or siblings have failed to make him feel wanted, accepted, and loved, he will grow up

2 For a detailed explanation of the main human needs and the healing work of the Trinity in this respect, refer to *The Inner Man: Spiritual Growth* by the author (Shine International Publications). The discussion here is only a brief overview to help us perceive God as a Trinity and understand our dire need for the work of the Trinity in our lives.

lacking a sense of belonging. Even when a family tries to offer this acceptance and love, it is sometimes done in a way that does not fulfil one's deep need for belonging. As a result, one may suffer from a sense of rejection and believe that he is not accepted, consequently leading to various types of behaviours and emotions, such as anger, anxiety, stress, and even violence.

Some people may try to compensate for this need by focusing on their outer appearance and possessions such as clothes, furniture, cars, manner of speech, or conduct. For example, they may dress excessively or buy expensive, flashy cars to attract attention. Some may even speak or act violently as a way of proving their existence and to draw the attention of others. These kinds of behaviours reflect the person's reaction to the neglect and lack of acceptance that he suffered from as a child, and his attempt to compensate for this unfulfilled need after growing up. Of course, this is an unhealthy behaviour or response that has negative consequences.

- The lack of fulfilment of the need to be valued and the need to have inner peace results in a guilty conscience, which may, in turn, lead to a sense of inferiority.

A person suffering from a lack of fulfilment of this need often tries to search for means of compensation. In order not to reveal his inferior self to others, this person may outwardly put on a different personality to hide his real self. Thus, when he is with people, he speaks and acts in a certain way that is not his true self. Then, when he is at home alone, he realises that he is estranged from himself, but cannot exist otherwise because he does not want to reveal his true inner self to others. Sometimes one does not even know why he behaves in such a way.

This picture or kind of behaviour is often the result of having had a guilty conscience for an extended period that has led to a sense of inferiority in certain areas, a sense of superiority in other areas, and even a sense of self-rejection. Consequently, one presents a fake personality before others, while his true personality, which is full of groaning and suffering, remains hidden inside him because of his guilty conscience and the lack of a deep sense of peace.

Only when one's conscience experiences true forgiveness can he experience true and profound peace. Experiencing forgiveness is a deep human need because man is created to be righteous. However, since we fail to live in righteousness, we suffer from a sense of guilt.

- The lack of fulfilment of the need for competency causes the person to have fear as a defence mechanism, leading to various behaviours and emotions, including:
    - Feeling tense, scared, or anxious while working
    - Always expecting failure in the results
    - Feeling frustrated, losing hope, and feeling depressed
    - Suffering from a sense of a lack of fulfilment

Why do human beings have these needs?

Each of these human needs reflects God's mind towards man:

- God created man *to belong to a family* and be a member of a family.
- God created man *to live in righteousness and holiness*, reflecting God's nature, because man is the image of God. God is righteous[3] and holy; therefore, man should also be righteous and holy, as the Scripture says: *'Be holy, for I am holy'* (1 Peter 1:16).
- God created man with a mission on earth for the sake of extending and proclaiming God's Kingdom.

---

3 Deuteronomy 32:4; Psalms 92:15

If one lacks the fulfilment of one or more of these needs, one feels lost and thus tries to compensate for what is lacking. However, these attempts at compensation are often more painful because they enter the person into vicious circles.

What is the solution?

The ultimate solution is in God, who revealed Himself as a Trinity; He fills and satisfies all the essential human needs. Each Person of the Trinity satisfies one of these main needs.

- The Person of the Father fulfils man's deep need to belong.
- The Person of the Son fulfils man's need to be valued, and his need for peace and forgiveness. These two needs are closely linked and are considered one main need for two reasons. Firstly, man experiences a lack of a sense of worth when he loses his peace. Peace here does not refer to the general peace but to the kind of peace that Jesus, the Son of God, grants to believers, as He says in John 14:27. Receiving this peace is related to our life in Christ and our fellowship with Him. This kind of peace gives the person a sense of value in his own eyes and in the eyes of others because it restores to him his true value in Christ. The other reason for the connection between these two needs is that *guilt* is one of the main defence mechanisms resulting from the lack of fulfilment of *the need for worth,* and the solution for guilt is to receive peace and experience forgiveness through the salvific work of the Son, as we will explain shortly.
- The Person of the Holy Spirit reveals to each person his mission and role in life and enables him to accomplish this role step by step, from one phase to the other.

How does this happen practically?

· The Person of the Father fills man's need to belong

A father shelters, protects, cares, and looks after his child. He accepts him in his weakness and rejoices in him. Something deep within us seeks someone who can provide this and fulfil these needs. If they are satisfied, we will feel embraced and found.

God the Father fulfils this need! His divine arms embrace us, provide us shelter, and give us a sense of belonging. He rejoices in us. In Him, we feel loved, accepted, and wanted; we feel that we belong, and experience true warmth which surrounds and shelters us. We feel that we are persons, not things.

If one grows up in a home in which there is true sacrificial fatherhood and motherhood that reflects and imparts God's Fatherhood and Motherhood, this person will wake up every morning feeling a certain warmth that brings deep comfort. He will feel loved, wanted, protected, looked after, and have a sense of belonging.

The Fatherhood and Motherhood of God the Father, as revealed in Scripture:

> *Doubtless* ***You are our Father****, though Abraham was ignorant of us, and Israel does not acknowledge us.* ***You, O Lord, are our Father****; our Redeemer from Everlasting is Your name* (Isaiah 63:16).

> *As one whom his* ***mother comforts****, so I will comfort you; and you shall be comforted in Jerusalem* (Isaiah 66:13).

God has arranged for each child to have a mother and a father so that, through their relationship with God the Father, they can reflect and impart to their child the true character and Person of God the Father.

When the child grows up and develops spiritual insight, he perceives that his parents are but a small manifestation or reflection of the Heavenly Father who offers the full satisfaction, warmth, tenderness, and protection through His true and ultimate Fatherhood and Motherhood. Every morning, the divine hand of the Father tells us that we are wanted, accepted, deeply loved, that we belong to the Trinity and are members of the household of God.[4]

A child needs to hear from his parents that he is a loved and wanted member of the family. However, when he grows up, he realises that this is not sufficient because these needs are a reflection of a much bigger and eternal need. Outwardly, we have a body, a tent that we will take off, but inwardly we have an eternal spirit. We need love and tenderness, but this need can only be truly filled from within by God's eternal love and tenderness.

Some may have grown up in families where parents did not understand their responsibilities according to God's mind. As a result, they have unsatisfied needs. Unless these needs are dealt with and their wounds healed, they will continue to cause them an inner groaning that will reflect on their personalities, relationships, and future, no matter how cleverly they try to hide or overcome them.

If we desire to live the fullness of what we have been created for and complete our roles and responsibilities according to the divine will, our inner, hidden needs must be satisfied. Also, the inner wounds caused by their lack of fulfilment in childhood must be healed.

If parts of a plastic container are squeezed in, its shape and size change, and the container becomes unfit for its purpose or function. Similarly, if the size and shape of my inner vessel change due to these areas of unfulfilled needs, God cannot reveal to me the

---

4 Ephesians 2:19

full role that I am created for because it can only be accomplished through the full, restored size and shape of my vessel. Therefore, God will not request of me something that I am incapable of doing because of my vessel, which is partly squeezed or crushed. At the same time, I myself will be in agony and will have inner groaning due to having unreleased potentials which are suppressed by these distorted and constricted areas in my vessel.

When these areas and distortions are healed and restored, one experiences the fullness of peace and comfort, discovers his role, and accomplishes it. This role, as the Scripture highlights, is that we would be a praise on earth.

In Ephesians 2:10, we read:

> *For we are His workmanship, created in Christ Jesus for good works, which God prepared beforehand that we should walk in them.*

According to the original Greek, these words mean *we are created to be a poem or a praise.* The English word *poem* is derived from the ancient Greek word *ποίημα* (*poiēma*), which is used in this verse. The Greek word also has a creative quality.

In the Old Testament, we read that God often said to His people that He wanted them to be a song or a praise on earth. For instance, Zephaniah 3:19, 20 says:

> *"Behold, at that time I will deal with all who afflict you; I will save the lame, and gather those who were driven out;* ***I will appoint them for praise and fame*** *in every land where they were put to shame. At that time I will bring you back, even at the time I gather you; for* ***I will give you fame and praise*** *among all the peoples of the earth, when I return your captives before your eyes," Says the Lord.*

A song or a poem consists of *words* and a *melody*. God created each person to be a poem. This poem needs a melody to give it its beauty. Who composes the melody?

The Holy Spirit is the eternal melody; He composes a specific melody for every poem. He knows the melody of every believer. Therefore, our fellowship with the Holy Spirit is important, for He shows me what is within me and shows me the song imprinted on my spirit. He also tells me that this song is not only composed of words, but words that have a melody, and asks me to allow Him to make it a praise on earth.

When we give the Holy Spirit the lead, the melody is played and becomes a symphony that pleases God's heart and also pleases the person's heart.

People around us will also hear it. It will be light on earth and eternal comfort that shines from every believer. Each believer is a song or melody that differs from the others; there is no end to these melodies!

We will remain as an unsung poem or a melody that is not played until we are corrected and restored from within, and our deep inner needs are healed through the Trinity. The poem will then be discovered; the melody will be given; and our life will become a song that reflects the beauty and glory of God, allowing many in the world to come to know Him.

- **The Person of the Son fills man's need for peace and forgiveness**

Jesus Christ, the Son, has granted us peace and forgiveness through His redemption:

> *Having abolished in His flesh the enmity, that is, the law of commandments contained in ordinances, so as to create in Himself one new man from the two,* ***thus making peace*** (Ephesians 2:15).

> *And by Him to reconcile all things to Himself, by Him, whether things on earth or things in heaven,* ***having made peace through the blood of His Cross*** (Colossians 1:20).

The work of redemption of the Son on the Cross is transferred to us through the Holy Spirit, purifying our conscience, washing away our guilt, and healing our hidden sins.

When hidden sins exist in the land of our souls, they can become pits, forming pockets of guilt within us. This guilt can be manifested in various ways, such as in conflicts, a sense of inferiority, or attempts to compensate for one's sense of lack. Guilt is the reason behind all these conflicts.

We desire to live in righteousness because something deep within us urges us to live this way. However, we frequently fail, and thus often feel that our lives are full of sins and shortcomings. This frustrates us and fills us with pockets of guilt and despair. This, in turn, is reflected in our relationships with others. It can also cause us to suffer self-rejection due to feeling that we are bad, defeated, and unable to be victorious.

The forgiveness of Christ, His love, and His redemption heal the guilt and transform the weakness and despair into strength and hope:

> *For God has not given us a spirit of fear, but of power and of love and of a sound mind* (2 Timothy 1:7).

But we also ought to forgive others, as the Scripture says:

> *And whenever you stand praying, if you have anything against anyone, forgive him, that your Father in heaven may also forgive*

you your trespasses. But if you do not forgive, neither will your Father in heaven forgive your trespasses (Mark 11:25, 26).

- **The Person of the Holy Spirit helps and enables us in all the above matters.**
  - He is all-powerful. He is tender. He is the eternal melody.
  - He is the living and cleansing waters.
  - He is the Lord, the Giver of Life.
  - He is the companion who comforts us and walks with us in our sojourning.
  - He is the *Paraclete* who defends us before our enemy, the accuser.
  - Through Him, we have fellowship with the Father and the Son.
  - He transfers to us the Fatherhood and Motherhood of God the Father, and hence our needs are fulfilled and our wounds healed. He transfers to us the warmth of the Father and surrounds us with it.
  - The Holy Spirit transfers to us the divine plan—the role that God the Father has appointed for each person. The Son has reconciled[5] us to the Father, allowing this role to be granted to us and making it possible for us to discover it. The Holy Spirit opens our eyes to see this role and mission. After we see it, the Holy Spirit enables us to accomplish it. He is our strength. He walks with us and fulfils this mission through us. He accompanies us every day.
  - He dwells in us and walks with us, granting us His sweet and comforting companionship.

5 2 Corinthians 5:18, 19; Colossians 1:20

- He is the divine energy or *dynamo* [Greek: δύναμις, *dynamis*[6]], as it says in the Book of Acts (for example, Acts 1:8; 3:12; 4:7,33; 6:8; 8:10; 10:38).
- He generates energy when we feel cold and frustrated.
- He is the Generator of love when we feel unable to love others.
- He is the Generator of life when the death that is deep within us manifests and imposes itself on us.
- He is the Generator of capability when we feel unable, crippled, and that things are beyond our ability, and that we cannot deal with them.
- He is the continuous Generator of all the things we need. These things have already been granted to us through the wells of salvation,[7] and the Holy Spirit transfers them to us.

This is God the Trinity whom we often fail to understand and know!

- He is the final and ultimate answer for the broken and destroyed humanity.
- The ultimate restoration, satisfaction, and correction of the human soul is through the Trinity.
- He should be our boasting and proclamation to a world that has rejected the Trinity or stumbled in Him.
- Wherever man is, and whatever he believes, his inner depth will continue to need and call upon God the Trinity.

---

6 DBL Greek, s.v. 'δύναμις.'

7 Isaiah 12:3

Finally, let us conclude this point with the passage in Ephesians 1:3–14:

> *Blessed be the God and Father of our Lord Jesus Christ, who has blessed us with every spiritual blessing in the heavenly places in Christ, just as He chose us in Him before the foundation of the world, that we should be holy and without blame before Him in love, having predestined us to adoption as sons* [The reference here is to the Father] *by Jesus Christ to Himself, according to the good pleasure of His will,* ***to the praise of the glory of His grace****, by which He made us accepted in the Beloved* [The Beloved is Jesus; since we are in Jesus, the Father looks upon us as beloved and as His children]. *In Him we have redemption through His blood, the forgiveness of sins,* [The reference here is to the Son who grants forgiveness of sins] *according to the riches of His grace which He made to abound toward us in all wisdom and prudence, having made known to us the mystery of His will, according to His good pleasure which He purposed in Himself, that in the dispensation of the fullness of the times He might gather together in one all things in Christ, both which are in heaven and which are on earth—in Him. In Him also we have obtained an inheritance, being predestined according to the purpose of Him who works all things according to the counsel of His will, that we who first trusted in Christ should be* ***to the praise of His glory****. In Him you also trusted, after you heard the word of truth, the gospel of your salvation; in whom also, having believed, you were sealed with the Holy Spirit of promise, who is the guarantee of our inheritance* [The reference here is to the Holy Spirit who works in us, allowing us to receive a foretaste of eternal life] *until the redemption of the purchased possession,* ***to the praise of His glory****.*

Notice the use of the phrase *to the praise of the glory* three times in this passage; each mention of the phrase refers to one of the Persons of the Trinity:

- Verse 6: *'To the praise of the glory of His grace'*—the reference is to the Father
- Verse 12: *'To the praise of His glory'*—the reference is to the Son
- Verse 14: *'To the praise of His glory'*—the reference is to the Holy Spirit

This is the revelation of the Trinity in this passage.

GOD THE FATHER

As we pray and read the Word of God, the Holy Spirit progressively reveals to us the correct vision of God, imprinting it in our hearts and minds, rectifying our distorted vision of Him, and completing what is missing in it.

Since the scope of this vision and revelation about God the Father is broad, in this study, we will only highlight a few foundational points about God the Father by looking at some revelations about Him in Scripture.

The fellowship with God the Father is sweet and wonderful, and genuinely fills man's deep, inner needs. However, we often have misconceptions about God that hinder us from entering into a true and deep fellowship with Him. He desires a true fellowship with us and seeks to correct our misconceptions about Him. Therefore, it is important to understand the divine biblical revelation about God and then turn it into principles that we adhere to, and then change our thinking accordingly. In other words, we need to understand it correctly and apply it correctly.

Though we may not admit it, sometimes we are afraid of God due to the false and distorted things we have been told about Him. One of these misconceptions is that when a crisis or a problem occurs in our life, God has allowed it and that it will work for the good. When people tell us such things, our minds become filled with the conviction that God allows sudden crises and dangers. We may even think that God is the One who causes these sudden, unpleasant situations and circumstances.

However, the truth that the Scriptures reveal is that God loves us unconditionally; He is good, and His mercy endures forever:

For the Lord is good; His mercy is everlasting (Psalm 100:5).

It is also written that the will of God is *'good and acceptable and perfect'* (Romans 12:2).

The Scriptures also reveal the following about God:

· God's ways are upright, just, and righteous

To declare that the Lord is upright; He is my rock, and there is no unrighteousness in Him (Psalm 92:15).

Yet you say, 'The way of the Lord is not fair.' Hear now, O house of Israel, is it not My way which is fair, and your ways which are not fair? (Ezekiel 18:25).

· God gives life

I have come that they may have life, and that they may have it more abundantly (John 10:10).

· God satisfies us and He is our delight

*You open Your hand and **satisfy** the desire of every living thing* (Psalm 145:16).

*I shall be **satisfied** when I awake in Your likeness* (Psalm 17:15).

· Everything that comes from God brings the fullness of joy and is delightful

In Your presence is fullness of joy; at Your right hand are pleasures forevermore (Psalm 16:11).

- God is good and has prepared all good things for us, even beyond our imagination and expectation

  Eye has not seen, nor ear heard, nor have entered into the heart of man the things which God has prepared for those who love Him (1 Corinthians 2:9).

If this is what the Scriptures tell us about God, we ought not be confused or perplexed when adverse circumstances occur, but rather proclaim the truth revealed in God's Word.

In James 1:13, 14, we read:

> *Let no one say when he is tempted, "I am tempted by God"; for God cannot be tempted by evil,* ***nor does He Himself tempt anyone****. But each one is tempted when he is drawn away by his own desires and enticed.*[8]

A question may arise in this respect:

If adverse circumstances do not come from God, what causes them?

As we journey on earth, two sources can be at work in our lives: God or the devil.

The devil is a thief who comes to steal, kill, and destroy (John 10:10). He was a murderer from the beginning and is a liar and the father of it (John 8:44). The ways of the enemy are deceitful because he is a liar.

On the other hand, as we have understood from the biblical revelation, God is good, merciful, upright, and just. He leads us in straight paths and fills our lives with goodness, day after day.

---

8 This truth is different from the truth about suffering, which will be explained shortly.

Therefore, if something destructive, deceitful, and crooked occurs in our lives, we can be assured that these are the typical ways of the enemy.

What gives the enemy a chance to interfere in our lives in such a way?

The Bible describes the path of following Christ as entering through the narrow gate (Matthew 7:13, 14; Luke 13:24). As long as we are watchful and continually walk in this narrow path of following the Lord, we are on a safe path, for the good hand of God will be stretched over us. Nehemiah speaks of the hand of God that had been good upon him (Nehemiah 2:18). As long as the good hand of God is stretched over us, it protects us, as the Psalm says:

> *For He shall give His angels charge over you, to keep you in all your ways. In their hands they shall bear you up, lest you dash your foot against a stone* (Psalm 91:11, 12).

If we cling to God and submit to His will, He leads us in straight paths, protects us, and gives us abundant life.

However, if we deviate from this straight and safe path, which sometimes happens even without us noticing it due to our lack of watchfulness, we will be more exposed to the hand of the devil and his principalities. As a result, we may face problems, doors may be closed to us, and many things in our lives may be confused and in a mess. This situation reflects the hand of the enemy at work; it is not the good hand of God. When the enemy extends his hand to do evil work, he tries to deceive us, making us believe that God has forsaken us. Therefore, it is important to discern correctly and to have a correct vision of God and of the enemy.

When our vision of God is corrected and our relationship with Him is restored, we will daily expect good things, knowing that His mercies are new every morning, as the Scripture says:

> *Through the Lord's mercies we are not consumed, because His compassions fail not. They are* ***new every morning****; Great is Your faithfulness* (Lamentations 3:22, 23).

Why does God allow this evil hand of the enemy to reach us, and why does He remain silent?

God is righteous, and everything in His Kingdom is orderly and follows certain rules and principles.

If we walk in His path, His hand will be stretched over us; however, if we are derailed from this path and persistently deviate from it, He does not prevent or force us for two reasons:

- *God gave us free will*

God has given man freedom to choose. If we walk faithfully in His path, He embraces us. However, if we deviate from His path, though He will still be close to us, He will not compel us against our choice. This does not mean that He forsakes us. Rather, He continues to warn us once and twice, but we often fail to notice or perceive His warnings. It is written: *'For God speaks in one way, and in two, though man does not perceive it'* (Job 33:14, ESV).

- *Since the devil is the one who deceives us, if God comes after us, the devil will ask God to give him his chance and be fair to him*

We learn this from the Book of Job (Job 1:6–12) when the devil went to God and said to Him that Job was righteous because He (God) blessed him and made a hedge around him. He then asked God to give him a chance to touch all that Job had, and said that then Job would surely blaspheme. God allowed Satan to touch all that Job had, but He put limitations on Satan. Satan thus tempted Job in various ways, but Job was finally approved, and the devil was put to shame. We then read that *'the Lord blessed the latter days of Job more than his beginning'* (Job 42:12).

An important note about suffering

As we said, there are instances when God's people are negligent and not watchful, and thus can gradually deviate from His path, even without noticing it. If they neglect His warnings and persist in their deviation, they may face difficulties or catastrophic events, having come out of the protection of the good hand of God that is stretched over those who walk in the straight path. However, there are other instances when we may go through suffering and difficulties without deviating from God's path. These kinds of suffering are different, and God sometimes allows them for a purpose. However, He is not the One who brings evil, and He turns these difficult situations for our good and benefit. For example, these situations may be tools for sanctification, purification, reshaping, or preparation for ministry.[9] They can also be a fellowship in His sufferings, to which we are called, as we read in Philippians 3:10:

> *That I may know Him and the power of His resurrection, and the* ***fellowship of His sufferings****, being conformed to His death.*

They can even be persecutions or unfair accusations that approve us and become a testimony to others of our love of Jesus, hence bringing many souls to Christ, as was the case with the martyrs, saints, and Fathers of the Church.

9 For example, He allowed Joseph to be unfairly imprisoned, yet He was with him and used this situation to prepare him for the mission ahead.

Another point that we need to learn about God the Father:

When we learn to enter into true fellowship with the Father, we will experience His divine bosom, which is full of love and life, embracing all who draw near Him. We will experience being encompassed in the abundance of life, love, warmth, and strength. We will experience heaven while still living on earth.

As mentioned earlier, God is a Father (Isaiah 63:16) and a Mother (Isaiah 66:12, 13); therefore, He wants to pour out His love upon us, carry us, and comfort us. We often live in spiritual poverty because we worship God with a spirit of slavery, not with the spirit of adoption (Ephesians 1:5). However, the truth that the Scriptures reveal is that He is our Father, and we are His children:

> *But as many as received Him, to them He gave the right* ***to become children of God****, to those who believe in His name* (John 1:12).

> *For you* ***did not receive the spirit of slavery*** *to fall back into fear, but you have* ***received the Spirit of adoption*** *as sons, by whom we cry, "Abba! Father!"* (Romans 8:15, ESV).

When we enter into this true level of fellowship with the Father, enter His bosom, and receive His warmth and love, we can present and radiate it to others. It will shine in our words, and we will become life-bearers.

To sum up, we ought to change our vision and expectations based on what the Scriptures reveal about God the Father.

The Scriptures reveal that:

- God the Father is the divine bosom that desires to embrace all His children

When He embraces us, our sins and burdens dissolve and spontaneously fall off our shoulders because He forgives and forgets:

> *For I will forgive their iniquity, and their sin I will remember no more* (Jeremiah 31:34).

- He desires to wash us from our sins

He does not wait for us to go to Him when we are good and perfect. Rather, if we fall, and then get up, and go to Him, He will cleanse us and forgive our sins:

> *Purge me with hyssop, and I shall be clean; wash me, and I shall be whiter than snow. Make me hear joy and gladness, that the bones You have broken may rejoice* (Psalm 51:7, 8).

> *For a righteous man may fall seven times and rise again, but the wicked shall fall by calamity* (Proverbs 24:16).

- He is the Fatherly Shepherd who cares for us and is pleased to give us good gifts every day

> *If a son asks for bread from any father among you, will he give him a stone? Or if he asks for a fish, will he give him a serpent instead of a fish? Or if he asks for an egg, will he offer him a scorpion? If you then, being evil, know how to give good gifts to your children, how much more will your heavenly Father give the Holy Spirit to those who ask Him!* (Luke 11:11–13).

- He defends us against our enemies because He is a mighty God

> *Let the words of my mouth and the meditation of my heart be acceptable in Your sight, O Lord,* ***my strength and my Redeemer*** (Psalm 19:14).

The word *Redeemer* is repeated numerously throughout the Bible; it refers to the fullness of the protection we need.

- He has prepared for us an eternal inheritance in heaven

This is but a glimpse about the Father.

THE SON
JESUS CHRIST

Jesus is a *mystery* and a *revelation.*

· Jesus is the mystery of God

> *That their hearts may be encouraged, being knit together in love, and attaining to all riches of the full assurance of understanding, to the knowledge of* ***the mystery of God****, both of the Father and of Christ* (Colossians 2:2).

He is in the bosom of the Father and is united with Him. Yet, He came out of this bosom and was incarnated to reveal the Father to us:

> *No one has seen God at any time.* ***The only begotten Son, who is in the bosom of the Father,*** *He has declared Him* (John 1:18).

> *I came forth from the Father and have come into the world. Again, I leave the world and go to the Father* (John 16:28).

> *Now to Him who is able to establish you according to my gospel and the preaching of Jesus Christ,* ***according to the revelation of the mystery kept secret since the world began but now made manifest****, and by the prophetic Scriptures made known to all nations, according to the commandment of the everlasting God, for obedience to the faith* (Romans 16:25, 26).

· Jesus is our salvation and redemption

> *In Him we have redemption through His blood, the forgiveness of sins, according to the riches of His grace* (Ephesians 1:7).

Thus, Jesus is the mystery who *revealed the Father* and who *revealed our salvation and redemption.*

Since Jesus is the Word, the Logos, we need to go through the books of Scripture, the Word, to learn more about Him.

A brief journey through the books of Scripture from Genesis to Revelation to see how Christ is revealed in them:

- **In the Books of Moses, Christ is the Word of God who completed the act of Creation**

God created the world through His Word. He said: *'Let there be ...'*, and *there was.*

We said that Christ is *a mystery* and *a revelation*. The first revelation is that He is the Word proceeding from the mouth of God, creating the world:

> *For* ***by Him all things were created*** *that are in heaven and that are on earth, visible and invisible, whether thrones or dominions or principalities or powers.* ***All things were created through Him and for Him*** (Colossians 1:16).

In the Book of Proverbs, we read:

> *Then* ***I was beside Him as a master craftsman****; and I was daily His delight, rejoicing always before Him, rejoicing in His inhabited world, and my delight was with the sons of men* (Proverbs 8:30, 31).

Here Christ is speaking in the personified form as 'Wisdom'. Christ is Wisdom:

> *You are in Christ Jesus, who* ***became for us wisdom from God****— and righteousness and sanctification and redemption* (1 Corinthians 1:30).

There is no separation between the Word of God and the Wisdom of God because, when God speaks, Wisdom comes out of His mouth. Thus, Christ is the *Word of God* and the *Wisdom of God.*

Christ is also the *Power of God* who performed all of God's will and plans through His redemptive work:

> *But to those who are called, both Jews and Greeks,* ***Christ the power of God and the wisdom of God*** (1 Corinthians 1:24).

Thus, Christ is the Word, the Wisdom, and the Power of God. He created the cosmos, ordained the plans for it, and came to save it. Therefore, if anyone wants to discover God's plan for his life, the key to entering into this plan is through Christ, the Word and Wisdom of God:

> *For we are His workmanship,* ***created in Christ Jesus for good works,*** *which God prepared beforehand that we should walk in them* (Ephesians 2:10).

- **In the Book of Psalms, we read about Christ the Saviour and Redeemer**

Redemption was revealed in the Old Testament, even before its manifestation in the New Testament. In the Psalms, we read about the Messiah, the Redeemer, and the Saviour who not only saves us from sins and spiritual weaknesses but also saves and delivers us from difficult circumstances, problems, tribulations, and all the evil plans of the devil. The problems that we face and from which the Messiah saves us are often both internal and external, with a frequent correlation between them. They are usually caused by the devil (external) and our fallen nature (internal). Therefore, the more we receive the redemptive work of Christ in our inner lives, the more our outer circumstances are resolved. To the extent that we receive from Christ's redemptive work, a certain spiritual sphere envelops us, and we become surrounded by angels and the divine presence. In such a sphere, even if we face difficult circumstances, they do not easily shake us.

The Psalmist spoke about Christ the Redeemer and Saviour in Psalm 103:4, saying: *'Who **redeems your life from destruction,** Who crowns you with lovingkindness and tender mercies.'*

All the generations of the Old Testament waited for the Messiah and sang their Psalms and praises to Him. Hannah, Samuel's mother, was the first to speak about the Messiah in her praise, which the Virgin Mary later quoted parts of.

- **The prophets also spoke about Christ**

Each prophet had a certain perspective of Christ and reflected it in his prophecy.

Zechariah saw the facet of His gentleness and tenderness, seeing Him as wine and grain

> ***Grain** shall make the **young men** thrive, and **new wine** the **young women*** (Zechariah 9:17).

These mystical words convey an important divine truth:

Adam was created to be the power of God, who performs God's plans on earth, and Eve was created to be the delight of God on earth and to help Adam with the hardships he faces, renewing his energy and strength.

However, when sin entered, Adam became a god who wanted to dominate others, and Eve became a stumbling block. Therefore, Zechariah says that the Redeemer would come and restore creation to its first beauty and glory. He would offer Himself as *grain* that would nourish the new Adam—the redeemed man. This redeemed man (the new Adam) would feed on Christ. As a result, the new inner man would grow and be strengthened, and thus be able to accomplish God's plan on earth. Christ the Redeemer is also the wine that Eve would drink and thus be filled with joy and delight. As a result, she would become the delight of God on earth and lift the hardships of Adam. In John 6, Jesus says:

> *For **My flesh is food indeed, and My blood is drink indeed.** He who eats My flesh and drinks My blood abides in Me, and I in him. As the living Father sent Me, and I live because of the Father, so he who feeds on Me will live because of Me. This is the bread which came down from heaven—not as your fathers ate the manna, and are dead. He who eats this bread will live forever* (John 6:55–58).

Micah saw Christ as the Ruler, *whose goings forth are from of old*

> *But you, Bethlehem Ephrathah, though you are little among the thousands of Judah, yet out of you shall come forth to Me **the One to be Ruler in Israel, whose goings forth are from of old, from everlasting*** (Micah 5:2).

No one is greater than Christ. He is the Ruler over the life of every believer. He has a special divine economy for each person, which transforms the person's life into a melody or poem sung on earth for the glory of God, proclaiming His beauty and goodness.

Micah also saw Christ as the Ruler of the nations, not only the Ruler of individual people. He is the King of all the kings of the earth. Through Him, the rulers can receive the wisdom that helps them govern their nations.

Jacob saw Him as *Shiloh*—the One who has all our matters in His hands

In Genesis 49:10, we read:

> *The sceptre shall not depart from Judah, nor the ruler's staff between his feet,* ***until Shiloh comes****. And to him shall be the obedience of nations* (LEB).

Our matters are in His hands, not in the hands of the people at work, or our managers, or superiors, as we often think. Our matters are in the hands of Jesus Christ alone, who is our Head.

Haggai saw Him as *the Desire of All Nations*

> *'I will shake all nations, and they shall come to* ***the Desire of All Nations****, and I will fill this temple with glory,' says the Lord of hosts* (Haggai 2:7).

The more we draw near to Him, the more we desire Him and love Him. Whenever His name is mentioned, He is desired by all.

Solomon saw Him as the Bridegroom

Solomon described Him, saying:

> *My beloved is white and ruddy, Chief among ten thousand* (Song of Solomon 5:10).

> *While the king is at his table, my spikenard sends forth its fragrance* (Song of Solomon 1:12).

Jesus is the Bridegroom who pours out His love upon His bride (the bride in Song of Solomon refers to each person[10] and to the Church).

10 Origen (2nd - 3rd centuries) and Gregory of Nyssa (4th century) consider that the Book of Song of Solomon applies to our spiritual relationship with Christ.

He made us and created us; therefore, He knows that our emotions can only be fulfilled and satisfied with a certain kind of love. He is Love incarnate, thus He pours into our hearts a kind of love that is not of this world. This love purifies us from the love of the world and from all artificial or false love. It is a special bridal love that satisfies our emotions.

God the Father offers us fatherly love that satisfies our deep inner needs that originate from the time of our birth, including our need to belong, to be looked after, and to receive tenderness. *Jesus offers bridal love* that satisfies our emotions and affections. The human emotions are satisfied only when the person receives genuine love, so as not to beg for false love from various sources. The more we beg for love, the more we are hurt. However, the bridal love of Jesus is rich and satisfying; if the human soul finds it and receives it, she does not seek any other love. The Book of Proverbs says: *'A satisfied soul loathes the honeycomb, but to a hungry soul every bitter thing is sweet'* (Proverbs 27:7).[11]

Christ in the New Testament

· Christ in the four Gospels

The Gospels portray Christ's manifold characteristics.

To complete redemption, it was necessary for Christ to assume human nature (Hebrews 2:14–17). However, this assumption of human nature had another purpose, which was to reveal the wholesome image of man, according to how God created man from the beginning, and to reveal the richness of the glory of this image, according to God's great wisdom. It was also to reveal

11 The meaning here is that a soul nourished by Christ's love is not ensnared by deceptive, worldly love, whereas an unfulfilled soul is easily deceived by/attracted to fleshly affection, leading to wounds and hardships.

God's manifold purposes through this image in which man was created.

This wholesome image of humanity that God originally created, and the manifold divine purposes of this image, are revealed through the diverse characteristics of Christ portrayed in the four Gospels. Each Evangelist saw a specific facet and focused on it in his Gospel.

- The Gospel of Matthew[12]

Apostle Matthew reveals the royal face of humanity that was lost and distorted by the fall. Thus, Christ is given the face of a Man,[13] a royal Man.

This royal face was originally Adam's face before the fall. Therefore, it is necessary to see this original image, which has become distorted by the fall, as one of the facets of the incarnate Christ, so that it may be restored to man and that we may see it and know it. At the same time, it helps us realise that this kingly image is man's original image as created by God, because God always wanted man to be a king. However, God does not want man to be a king according to the contemporary fallen design, which is often associated with control and arrogance. God has in His mind a completely different picture.

Christ revealed this design through His life on earth. Apostle Matthew then portrayed it in his Gospel. Thus, Apostle Matthew

---

12 This Gospel reveals Jesus the King and His Kingdom: for example, the parables of the Kingdom of heaven, and the manifesto of the Kingdom (the Sermon on the Mount).

13 It is known that the art symbols we see, especially in early iconography found in monasteries and ancient churches, specify one of the faces of the cherubim for each Gospel, as mentioned in the Book of Ezekiel and the Book of Revelation. Each of the four Evangelists was accompanied by an angelic power from the cherubic order to assist in writing the Gospel entrusted to him, thereby revealing a particular facet of the Person of Christ. For a detailed explanation of this point, refer to *Mysteries and Wonders in the Gospel of Mark* by the author (Shine International Publications).

commences his Gospel by saying: '*The book of the genealogy of Jesus Christ, the Son of David, the Son of Abraham*' (Matthew 1:1). This opening of the Gospel highlights Christ's royal kinship to King David.

Christ the King does not control or oppress human beings, as fallen kings do, but serves them with humility as the royal human in whom true and original humanity is revealed.

- The Gospel of Mark[14]

Apostle Mark reveals another characteristic of Christ in his Gospel, which is that of the Servant.

However, again, Christ's servitude does not conform to the current, distorted image that resulted from the fall, in which servitude is a symbol of weakness as the servant is usually humiliated, subjugated, and despised.

Isaiah (40–66) refers to the Messiah sent for salvation as the Lord's Suffering Servant. Throughout his Gospel, Apostle Mark describes Christ in His ministry as *the Servant* who came and emptied Himself to fulfil God's purposes of salvation (Philippians 2:5–11).

In order to reveal the corrected human image of the bondservant in the Person of Christ, Apostle Mark presents Christ as the Servant strengthened with the divine power, and who appears as one who is '*mighty to save*' (Isaiah 63:1). Therefore, Christ is given the image of *a lion* in this Gospel to help us understand that divine power accompanies this Servant (Christ) because He came to fulfil God's purposes. This image of Christ corrects the image of humiliation and subjugation associated with servitude.

---

14 This Gospel reveals the Servant of the Lord of whom Isaiah spoke; therefore, the Gospel begins by quoting from Isaiah 42:1–4.

This is how God willed man, the first Adam, to be when He created him. He wanted man to be a servant, but with humility and contrition rather than a sense of inferiority. This correct and healthy attitude qualifies the person to receive the power of God and His companionship so that his entire ministry may be strengthened with power. Scripture tells us that the Lord dwells with and accompanies those who have a humble and contrite heart:

> *For thus says the High and Lofty One who inhabits eternity, whose name is Holy: "I dwell in the high and holy place,* ***with him who has a contrite and humble spirit****, to revive the spirit of the humble, and to revive the heart of the contrite ones"* (Isaiah 57:15).

Through this correct image of the Lord's servant, the work of God's Kingdom is accomplished:

> *Till they see the Kingdom of God present with power* (Mark 9:1).

> *For the Kingdom of God is not in word but in power* (1 Corinthians 4:20).

This image of Christ as a lion also highlights that, though the devil *'walks about like a roaring lion, seeking whom he may devour'* (1 Peter 5:8), *'the Lion of the tribe of Judah'* (Revelation 5:5) has all the power and authority to defeat the devil.

- The Gospel of Luke[15]

Apostle Luke portrays another face of humanity, which is the face of the Priest who ministers to God on behalf of creation and on behalf of His brethren through sacrifice, worship, love, and gentleness, and with a true and wholesome humanity.

15 This Gospel speaks about priesthood and sacrifices, which were all revealed in Christ as their fulfilment.

Thus, Luke begins his Gospel with the topic of sacrifices. For example, the Gospel opens with Zacharias serving as a priest, and then proceeds to portray the sacrifices offered in the temple by the parents of Jesus.

The symbol of this Gospel is *an ox* because the ox is a well-known biblical reference to sacrifices. Offering sacrifices is the duty of priests and is part of the priesthood ministry. Though this ministry was carried out through the offerings of goats and calves in the Old Testament (Hebrews 9:12), in the New Testament it was elevated with *'better sacrifices than these'* (Hebrews 9:23), for we offer to God a sacrifice of praise, which is the fruit of our lips that confess His name, and do good and share with others (Hebrews 13:15, 16).

> *Not with the blood of goats and calves, but with His own blood He entered the Most Holy Place once for all, having obtained eternal redemption* (Hebrews 9:12).

> *Therefore by Him let us continually offer the sacrifice of praise to God, that is, the fruit of our lips, giving thanks to His name. But do not forget to do good and to share, for with such sacrifices God is well pleased* (Hebrews 13:15, 16).

Luke's Gospel is also characterised by gentleness and tenderness. He presents Jesus as being tender, and as one who has a priestly heart that carries humanity. Jesus is presented as a Friend of humanity and one who cares for the various sectors of society: men, women, and children. This is a unique feature of this Gospel.

He cared for the children. He also cared for women at a time when women were not respected or well-treated by society. He wanted to restore to women their dignity and honour, and to emphasise that there is no difference between male and female in honour. For example, He likened the Kingdom of God to yeast that a woman took and hid in three measures of wheat flour until the whole batch was leavened (Luke 13:21).[16]

Apostle Paul highlighted this principle in his Epistle to the Galatians, saying: *'**there is neither male nor female**; for you are all one in Christ Jesus'* (Galatians 3:28).

Also, in Genesis 1:27, we read: *'So God created man in His own image; in the image of God He created him; **male and female He created them**'*.

As mentioned earlier, God is a Father and a Mother; therefore, when He wanted to reflect His image in human beings, He created male and female as equals.

When Christ was incarnated to reveal God to us—for Christ is the image of God, as Apostle Paul highlighted in his Epistles to the Hebrews and the Colossians—He revealed to us that God created us in His image, and that men and women are equal. Therefore, He performed miracles with men and women, and with children, both boys and girls.

- The Gospel of John[17]

Apostle John reveals the mystery of partaking in the divine nature, which has been granted to humanity.

This does not mean that human beings become divine by nature, but that humanity has been granted the privilege of being in fellowship with God by grace, through a mystery. Our minds might not perceive this mystery fully, but we must accept it by faith. As

---

16 When we read the Gospels, in general, we notice that half the miracles of Christ were performed for men and half for women. He also performed miracles for children, both boys and girls. For example, He healed the epileptic son (Matthew 17:14–18) and the daughter of the Canaanite woman (Matthew 15:21–28). He came to the whole of creation.

17 This Gospel reveals Christ's divinity and His incarnation for the sake of completing our salvation.

we partake of the mystical divine food by eating the body of Christ and drinking His blood, eternal life flows in us:

> *Whoever eats My flesh and drinks My blood has eternal life, and I will raise him up at the last day. For My flesh is food indeed, and My blood is drink indeed. He who eats My flesh and drinks My blood abides in Me, and I in him. As the living Father sent Me, and I live because of the Father, so he who feeds on Me will live because of Me. This is the bread which came down from heaven—not as your fathers ate the manna, and are dead. He who eats this bread will live forever* (John 6:54–58).

John was thus given the image of *an eagle,* which means that he can soar in the realms of divinity. By this, the believer takes his new place in Jesus Christ in the heavenly places:

> *Which He worked in Christ when He raised Him from the dead and seated Him at His right hand* ***in the heavenly places*** (Ephesians 1:20).

> *And raised us up together, and made us sit together* ***in the heavenly places*** *in Christ Jesus* (Ephesians 2:6).

Therefore, the Gospel of John focuses on Christ's incarnated divinity—the God-Man (John 1:1–5, 14). When we read the Gospel of John, we perceive the divinity of Christ and, at the same time, we see the humanity of Christ to the extent that we as believers can put ourselves in the place of Christ and say the same words or pray the same prayers. For example, Jesus said: *'For this reason I was born, and for this reason I have come into the world'* (John 18:37). We, as believers, can say these same words when we discover God's purpose for our lives. Jesus also said: *'I have finished the work which You have given Me to do'* (John 17:4). Again, as believers, we ought to know the work that has been given to us and continue to do it until we complete it and enter our rest.

Christ the Son came to show us how a son of God must live. He made us children of God so that we can follow in His footsteps, pray His prayers, and take our place in God—our heavenly Father—like the Son who is in the bosom of the Father. Therefore, in the opening chapter of the Gospel of John, we read: *'But as many as received Him, to them He gave the right to become children of God'* (John 1:12).

· In the Book of Acts, Christ is a Message

The Book of Acts mainly speaks about the Church, but it also reveals Christ as a *message*:

> *For there is no other name under heaven given among men by which we must be saved* (Acts 4:12).

Christ is a message of redemption and salvation. He is a message of life, truth, and the way, for He is the Way, the Truth, and the Life (John 14:6). He is a message that we should live out, proclaim, and preach:

> ***Him we preach,*** *warning every man and teaching every man in all wisdom, that we may present every man perfect in Christ Jesus* (Colossians 1:28).

> *Through Him we have received grace and* ***apostleship*** (Romans 1:5).

He is a message of which we ought to be proud.

· The Epistles

The Epistles help us understand the significance of the Tabernacle and its items. The Tabernacle symbolises Christ; it is the *'shadow of the heavenly things'* (Hebrews 8:5). Jesus is the manna, the Ark of the Covenant, the table of the showbread, the bronze altar (the mystery of His redemption), and the golden altar of incense (the mystery of His intercessory prayers). In the New Testament, these shadows and symbols have been revealed; *Christ became the Head of the Church* (Colossians 2:19) and the food that nourishes the Church.

The Epistles speak about the Church of Christ, highlighting that Christ is the Head of the Church and the author and finisher of her faith (Hebrews 12:2). As the Church sojourns in the world, Christ accompanies her until she completes her role and mission on earth.

In His second coming, Christ will be proclaimed and revealed as the Bridegroom of the Church, and the Church will be His glorified Bride. This will be the marriage supper of the Lamb (Revelation 19:7). Jesus will be proclaimed as King over all the earth. The full power of His redemption and glory will be revealed and manifested. He will present us to the Father as His Bride who is united with Him, of His flesh and of His bones, *'not having spot or wrinkle or any such thing, but ... holy and without blemish'* (Ephesians 5:27, 30), holy like Him because He is holy. At this point, God will become all in all, as we read in 1 Corinthians 15:24–28:

> *Then comes the end, when He delivers the Kingdom to God the Father, when He puts an end to all rule and all authority and power. For He must reign till He has put all enemies under His feet. The last enemy that will be destroyed is death. For "He has put all things under His feet." But when He says "all things are put under Him," it is evident that He who put all things under Him is excepted. Now when all things are made subject to Him, then the Son Himself will also be subject to Him who put all things under Him,* ***that God may be all in all.***

Thus, the story will end as it began, with God being revealed as all in all. The Trinity was revealed, and His plans were revealed, but the enemy interfered, and the fall happened. However, redemption was manifested. Therefore, God's plans and purposes will be fulfilled and completed, and God's Kingdom will be proclaimed and manifested. The Bride who is united with the Bridegroom will be revealed and presented to the Father so that God may once again be all in all.

This was a brief overview of Christ as revealed in the books of the Scripture from Genesis to Revelation. When we perceive this correct vision of Christ and seek Him, we will find Him as the mystery of our lives, who fills our hearts and revives us. Thus, our whole life becomes His, belonging to Him, because He has bought us with His blood. When we follow Him and enter into fellowship with Him, our lives become meaningful.

The Person and Work of Christ

The New Testament highlights two important aspects of Christ:

- The Person of Christ
- The Work of Christ

The New Testament presents to us the Person of Christ and His manifold characteristics, so that His image may be imprinted within us and we may follow in His footsteps. He is our example and the living image into which we ought to be transformed: *'To be conformed to the image of His Son, that He might be the firstborn among many brethren'* (Romans 8:29).

The New Testament also highlights the work of Christ—His redemption. The more we receive from this work of redemption in our inner man, the more we will be enabled to follow Christ and be transformed into His image.

The Person of Christ is highlighted in the Gospels, while His work of redemption is mainly highlighted in the Epistles.

- **The Person of the Son and His characteristics are highlighted in the Gospels**

The Gospels outline the footsteps of Jesus and reveal to us how He lived His days on earth—His work and His conduct.

We are called to walk as He walked (1 John 2:6). Therefore, every time we read the Gospels, we need to ask Him to help us see His Person and how He lived.

As we read the words of the Gospels, we ought to chew on them, meditate on them, eat them, drink them, and talk of them when we lie down and when we rise up (Deuteronomy 6:7). As we do so, the Holy Spirit gradually opens our minds and understanding to know the Person of Christ. The more the eyes of our minds are opened and see Him, the more we can be transformed into His image.

Therefore, we should not think of the Gospels as stories that we have read before and already know. They indeed present a Living, Divine, Incarnated Person who walked in our world. He entered our fallen world to give it light and to give life to the dead. He emptied Himself and took our human form. Thus, when we look at Him, by His grace we can see and anticipate how we will look when we are cleansed and healed from the effects of the fall.

Also, as we read the Gospels, we must bend our knees, asking Him to pour the mystery of His life into us so that we can live as He lived. Since we are the children of God, we ought to do as the Son did when He was incarnated and lived on earth, so that the Father may be pleased with us, and that we may fulfil His will: '*Your will be done on earth as it is in heaven*' (Matthew 6:10).

We can see in Christ how a wholesome and perfect humanity lives, fulfilling the will of the Father. Seeing and perceiving this helps us to follow in His footsteps, imitate Him, and do as He did. Though our humanity is not perfect, unlike Christ's perfect humanity, it can be redeemed through His redemptive work. Consequently, we can do as He did, not out of our own ability but through His grace which strengthens us and the work of His Spirit.

Jesus is our door to the Father and to our fellowship with the Father. We have the right to this fellowship with the Father through the adoption granted to us in Christ (Ephesians 1:5). Similarly, we can have fellowship with the Holy Spirit through Christ, who has redeemed us. The manifestation of Christ's redemptive work within us allows the Holy Spirit to come and dwell in us and become our companion and comforter. In the Old Testament, oil was poured after the blood of sacrifices was shed. In the same way, after the crucifixion and the completion of Christ's redemptive work, the Holy Spirit was poured upon the disciples on the Day of Pentecost.

Thus, through Christ, we know our heavenly Father and experience the companionship of the Holy Spirit. Christ is the door. He is the beginning and the end, as He said: *'I am the Alpha and the Omega, the Beginning and the End'* (Revelation 1:8). He is all in all. He is the reason for our life. He is our Redeemer. We are a fallen humanity, and our only hope is in Christ—the hope of glory (Colossians 1:27).

· **The Book of Acts speaks about the Church**

The Book of Acts falls between the Gospels, which reflect the Person of Christ, and the Epistles, which speak about the redemptive work of Christ.

The Book of Acts tells us how the Church was established and originally lived, so that we can live in the same way as the apostolic Church. As we read this book of Scripture, we see how the

Church served the nations, was persecuted, suffered, overcame Satan, and spread light and life on earth.

The Church ought to proclaim Christ's redemption and be the representative of Christ on earth. Since the Church is Christ's body, she ought to do what He wants her to do, and proclaim to humanity, which is living in darkness, sin, and death, the message of hope, saying: *'Arise, shine; there is life and light.'*

This message should be proclaimed not only through words but through the testimony of a holy and humble life, which is ready to sacrifice to the point of death for the sake of others.

Scripture says:

> *And they overcame him by the blood of the Lamb and by the* ***word of their testimony****, and they* ***did not love their lives to the death*** (Revelation 12:11).

If we desire to proclaim the mystery of Christ to others, we must walk the path that He walked. As He died, we should also be ready to die. We die through love, humility, accepting pain and suffering, and even shedding our blood. By this, we become the Church of Christ that can change the face of the earth.

- **The redemptive work of Christ, and how the Church ought to live through it, as highlighted in the Epistles**

Christ's redemptive work transforms the person and brings these redeemed people together, uniting them and making them a true Body that is united with the Head, Christ, thus becoming *a perfect man*, as we read in Ephesians:

> *Till we all come to the unity of the faith and of the knowledge of the Son of God,* ***to a perfect man****, to the measure of the stature of the fullness of Christ ...* [that we,] *speaking the truth in love, may*

> *grow up in all things into Him who is the head—Christ—from whom the whole body, joined and knit together by what every joint supplies, according to the effective working by which every part does its share, causes growth of the body for the edifying of itself in love* (Ephesians 4:13, 15, 16).

When this *perfect man* walks on earth, it is as if Christ Himself is walking on earth, and he fulfils all that Christ desires. Christ can do through His Church all that He did during His incarnation.

His Church ought to proclaim His redemption so that redemption may be manifested in every person, and that the kingdoms of this world may become the Kingdoms of our Lord and of His Christ (Revelation 11:15). By this, Christ the King would come again, and the Kingdom of God would be in our midst, as we pray in the Lord's Prayer: *'Your Kingdom come'* (Matthew 6:10).

The problem of the Church today is that she is not truly or correctly united with the Head—Christ. We ought to be united together and become members of one Body, because only a body can be united with the Head, not separate members. In order to be united members, each member should experience the work of redemption. The Holy Spirit then connects these redeemed members together, making them a Body that is ready to be united with the Head. As a result, life flows in this Body abundantly: *'It is like the precious oil upon the head, running down on the beard, the beard of Aaron, running down on the edge of his garments'* (Psalm 133:2). These garments extend to the world to proclaim to it the message of Christ.

Therefore, when we read the Epistles, we ought to look at the complete work of Christ. This includes the work of the Cross, the work of the blood of Jesus, the work of resurrection, the work of ascension, and the pouring of the Holy Spirit. We ought to learn how to benefit from this great divine work in order to be redeemed people and redeemed members of the Body, so that the Holy Spirit may unite us and make us into a living Body connected to the Head.

THE HOLY SPIRIT

Readings

▪ John 15:26, 27

But when the Helper comes, whom I shall send to you from the Father, the Spirit of truth who proceeds from the Father, He will testify of Me. And you also will bear witness, because you have been with Me from the beginning.

▪ 1 Corinthians 3:16, 17

Do you not know that you are the temple of God and that the Spirit of God dwells in you? If anyone defiles the temple of God, God will destroy him. For the temple of God is holy, which temple you are.

▪ 1 Corinthians 2:10–13

But God has revealed them to us through His Spirit. For the Spirit searches all things, yes, the deep things of God. For what man knows the things of a man except the spirit of the man which is in him? Even so no one knows the things of God except the Spirit of God. Now we have received, not the spirit of the world, but the Spirit who is from God, that we might know the things that have been freely given to us by God. These things we also speak, not in words which man's wisdom teaches but which the Holy Spirit teaches, comparing spiritual things with spiritual.

▪ 1 Corinthians 6:19

Or do you not know that your body is the temple of the Holy Spirit who is in you, whom you have from God, and you are not your own?

▪ 1 Corinthians 12–14

Chapter 12

Now concerning spiritual gifts, brethren, I do not want you to be ignorant: You know that you were Gentiles, carried away to these dumb idols, however you were led. Therefore I make known to you that no one speaking by the Spirit of God calls Jesus accursed, and no one can say that Jesus is Lord except by the Holy Spirit. There are diversities of gifts, but the same Spirit. There are differences of ministries, but the same Lord. And there are diversities of activities, but it is the same God who works all in all. But the manifestation of the Spirit is given to each one for the profit of all: for to one is given the word of wisdom through the Spirit, to another the word of knowledge through the same Spirit, to another faith by the same Spirit, to another gifts of healings by the same Spirit, to another the working of miracles, to another prophecy, to another discerning of spirits, to another different kinds of tongues, to another the interpretation of tongues. But one and the same Spirit works all these things, distributing to each one individually as He wills. For as the body is one and has many members, but all the members of that one body, being many, are one body, so also is Christ. For by one Spirit we were all baptized into one body—whether Jews or Greeks, whether slaves or free—and have all been made to drink into one Spirit. For in fact the body is not one member but many. If the foot should say, "Because I am not a hand, I am not of the body," is it therefore not of the body? And if the ear should say, "Because I am not an eye, I am not of the body," is it therefore not of the body? If the whole body were an eye, where would be the hearing? If the whole were hearing, where would be the smelling? But now God has set the members, each one of them, in the body just as He pleased. And if they were all one member, where would the body be? But now indeed there are many members, yet one body. And the eye cannot say to the hand, "I have no need of you"; nor again the head to the feet, "I have no need of you." No, much rather, those members of the body which seem to be weaker are necessary. And those members of the body which we think to be less honourable, on these we bestow greater honour; and our unpresentable parts have greater modesty, but our presentable parts have no need. But God composed the body, having given greater honour to that part which lacks it, that there should be no schism in the body, but that the members should have the same care for one another. And if one member suffers, all the members suffer with it; or if one member is honoured, all the members rejoice with it. Now you are the body of Christ, and members individually. And God has appointed these in the church: first apostles, second prophets, third teachers, after that miracles, then gifts of healings, helps, administrations, varieties of tongues. Are all apostles? Are all prophets? Are all teachers? Are all workers of miracles? Do all have gifts of healings? Do all speak with tongues? Do all interpret? But earnestly desire the best gifts. And yet I show you a more excellent way.

Chapter 13

Though I speak with the tongues of men and of angels, but have not love, I have become sounding brass or a clanging cymbal. And though I have the gift of prophecy, and understand all mysteries and all knowledge, and though I have all faith, so that I could remove mountains, but have not love, I am nothing. And though I bestow all my goods to feed the poor, and though I give my body to be burned, but have not love, it profits me nothing. Love suffers long and is kind; love does not envy; love does not parade itself, is not puffed up; does not behave rudely, does not seek its own, is not provoked, thinks no evil; does not rejoice in iniquity, but rejoices in the truth; bears all things, believes all things, hopes all things, endures all things. Love never fails. But whether there are prophecies, they will fail; whether there are tongues, they will cease; whether there is knowledge, it will vanish away. For we know in part and we prophesy in part. But when that which is perfect has come, then that which is in part will be done away. When I was a child, I spoke as a child, I understood as a child, I thought as a child; but when I became a man, I put away childish things. For now we see in a mirror, dimly, but then face to face. Now I know in part, but then I shall know just as I also am known. And now abide faith, hope, love, these three; but the greatest of these is love.

Chapter 14

Pursue love, and desire spiritual gifts, but especially that you may prophesy. For he who speaks in a tongue does not speak to men but to God, for no one understands him; however, in the spirit he speaks mysteries. But he who prophesies speaks edification and exhortation and comfort to men. He who speaks in a tongue edifies himself, but he who prophesies edifies the church. I wish you all spoke with tongues, but even more that you prophesied; for he who prophesies is greater than he who speaks with tongues, unless indeed he interprets, that the church may receive edification. But now, brethren, if I come to you speaking with tongues, what shall I profit you unless I speak to you either by revelation, by knowledge, by prophesying, or by teaching? Even things without life, whether flute or harp, when they make a sound, unless they make a distinction in the sounds, how will it be known what is piped or played? For if the trumpet makes an uncertain sound, who will prepare for battle? So likewise you, unless you utter by the tongue words easy to understand, how will it be known what is spoken? For you will be speaking into the air. There are, it may be, so many kinds of languages in the world, and none of them is without significance. Therefore, if I do not know the meaning of the language, I shall be a foreigner to him who speaks, and he who speaks will be a foreigner to me. Even so you, since you are zealous for spiritual gifts, let it be for the edification of the church that you seek to excel. Therefore let him who speaks in a tongue pray that he may interpret. For if I pray in a tongue, my spirit prays, but my understanding is unfruitful. What is the conclusion then? I will pray with the spirit, and I will also pray with the understanding. I will sing with the spirit, and I will also sing with the understanding. Otherwise, if you bless with the spirit, how will he who occupies the place of the uninformed say "Amen" at your giving of thanks, since he does not understand what you say? For you indeed give thanks well, but the other is not edified. I thank my God I speak with tongues more than you all; yet in the church I would rather speak five words with my understanding, that I may teach others also, than ten thousand words in a tongue. Brethren, do not be children in understanding; however, in malice be babes, but in understanding be mature. In the law it is written: "With men of other tongues and other lips I will speak to this people; And yet, for all that, they will not hear Me," says the Lord. Therefore tongues are for a sign, not to those who believe but to unbelievers; but prophesying is not for unbelievers but for those who believe. Therefore if the whole church comes together in one place, and all speak with tongues, and there come in those who are uninformed or unbelievers, will they not say that you are out of your mind? But if all prophesy, and an unbeliever or an uninformed person comes in, he is convinced by all, he is convicted by all. And thus the secrets of his heart are revealed; and so, falling down on his face, he will worship God and report that God is truly among you. How is it then, brethren? Whenever you come together, each of you has a psalm, has a teaching, has a tongue, has a revelation, has an interpretation. Let all things be done for edification. If anyone speaks in a tongue, let there be two or at the most three, each in turn, and let one interpret. But if there is no interpreter, let him keep silent in church, and let him speak to himself and to God. Let two or three prophets speak, and let the others judge. But if anything is revealed to another who sits by, let the first keep silent. For you can all prophesy one by one, that all may learn and all may be encouraged. And the spirits of the prophets are subject to the prophets. For God is not the author of confusion but of peace, as in all the churches of the saints. Let your women keep silent in the churches, for they are not permitted to speak; but they are to be submissive, as the law also says. And if they want to learn something, let them ask their own husbands at home; for it is shameful for women to speak in church. Or did the word of God come originally from you? Or was it you only that it reached? If anyone thinks himself to be a prophet or spiritual, let him acknowledge that the things which I write to you are the commandments of the Lord. But if anyone is ignorant, let him be ignorant. Therefore, brethren, desire earnestly to prophesy, and do not forbid to speak with tongues. Let all things be done decently and in order.

- **2 Corinthians 13:14**

The grace of the Lord Jesus Christ, and the love of God, and the communion of the Holy Spirit be with you all. Amen.

- **1 John 1:3**

That which we have seen and heard we declare to you, that you also may have fellowship with us; and truly our fellowship is with the Father and with His Son Jesus Christ.

- **1 John 5:6–8**

This is He who came by water and blood—Jesus Christ; not only by water, but by water and blood. And it is the Spirit who bears witness, because the Spirit is truth. For there are three that bear witness in heaven: the Father, the Word, and the Holy Spirit; and these three are one. And there are three that bear witness on earth: the Spirit, the water, and the blood; and these three agree as one.

The Holy Spirit is the great and amazing gift that the Father has granted us, as highlighted in the Book of Acts:

> *This Jesus God has raised up, of which we are all witnesses. Therefore being exalted to the right hand of God, and having* ***received from the Father the promise of the Holy Spirit, He poured out this which you now see and hear*** (Acts 2:32, 33).

The reference here is to the Day of Pentecost.

It may be easy to envision God the Father because we associate Him with the picture of an earthly father. We can also easily envisage the Son because we read about Him in the Gospels and see many icons of Him. However, it may not be easy to envision the Person of the Holy Spirit; therefore, we often think of Him as a power or an invisible Spirit.

He is indeed a power, but He is also a Person. Each Hypostasis of the Trinity is a Person having a distinct role, and, at the same time, they are in each other and are in unity as One God.

The Holy Spirit is the third Person of the Trinity. He walks with us. He is the *Paraclete,* meaning called alongside us as an advocate; therefore, He walks by our side and defends us against the adversary. He also *dwells in us*. Thus, He is *in us* and *beside us*. He wants to hold our hands and walk with us to show us the way and defend us when we face enemies along our journey.

The Psalmist says: *'Lead me, O Lord, in Your righteousness because of my enemies; make Your way straight before my face'* (Psalm 5:8). The Bible clearly highlights that those who walk in God's way face enemies who want to hinder them. These enemies are the devil and his evil powers.

The Holy Spirit also *'helps in our weaknesses'*:

> *Likewise the Spirit also* ***helps in our weaknesses****. For we do not know what we should pray for as we ought, but the Spirit Himself makes intercession for us with groanings which cannot be uttered* (Romans 8:26).

According to the original Greek, the phrase *'helps in our weaknesses'* signifies that He grasps our hand and walks with us, opening the way for us so that we can move forward.

The devil always tries to hinder any true spiritual steps in the lives of those who progressively grow in the spirit and move forward in fulfilling the divine purposes. However, the Holy Spirit comes to our aid, strengthening us, giving us power, and pushing the enemies out of our way.

We must learn the spiritual battles and how to deal with them, because the lack of understanding in this area can be one of the hindrances in our walk of following Christ. Therefore, one of the foundations in following Christ is to have a correct vision of our enemy, learn his strategies, and learn how to overcome him, as we will discuss later in this brief study. The Holy Spirit helps us in these battles of the enemy and helps us in all aspects. Therefore, we need to have true fellowship with the Holy Spirit.

We will discuss the topic of the Holy Spirit under five main headings:

1. The Holy Spirit and Our Fellowship with God
2. The Holy Spirit and the World
3. The Holy Spirit and the Church
4. The Holy Spirit and the Individual Person
5. The Holy Spirit and Ministry

1. The Holy Spirit and Our Fellowship with God

The Scripture commands us to *'**Grow** in the grace and knowledge of our Lord and Saviour Jesus Christ'* (2 Peter 3:18).

If we do not grow in knowing God, we will not be able to move forward steadily in our spiritual walk, nor bear a living message to the world and the people to whom we minister. This is simply because if we do not truly know God about whom we speak, we will only be repeating empty words that do not bear life. However, if we grow in knowing God, He will fill our hearts, stir our spirits, and fill our mouths with a living and anointed message.

The Holy Spirit is the Person of the Trinity who helps us know the Father and the Son and grow in our fellowship with God.

· The Holy Spirit reveals to us the Person of the Father

In Romans 8:16, we read:

> *The Spirit Himself bears witness with our spirit that we are children of God.*

Being children of God is not simply a fact that we know in our minds, but it is a truth to which the Holy Spirit bears witness in our spirit. He bears witness that we are children of God and that God is our Father.

We cannot know the Father merely through hearing words about Him and understanding them by our minds, but through an inner divine work of the Holy Spirit. The Holy Spirit stirs our hearts and opens our eyes to know our heavenly Father.

When the Holy Spirit reveals to us the Father who is full of love, tenderness, compassion, mercy, and care for us, we will rest in Him and feel secure in Him. We will know that we have a mighty, watchful, and faithful Father, and hence will be assured that nothing in our lives can happen randomly or adversely affect us. We will know that neither people nor evil powers can control our lives, nor are we handed over to circumstances—no matter how difficult the circumstances may seem.

We sometimes fail to know or be assured of this truth due to our lack of knowledge of the Fatherhood of God, His might, and His faithfulness. The enemy tries to hide this truth from our minds and eyes. Consequently, we remain ignorant of the Father and fail to enjoy His gifts.

The heavenly Father grants good gifts to His children, as we read in James 1:17: *'Every good gift and every perfect gift is from above, and comes down from the Father of lights, with whom there is no variation or shadow of turning.'*

We also read:

> *If you then, being evil, know how to give good gifts to your children, how much more will your Father who is in heaven give good things to those who ask Him!* (Matthew 7:11).

These gifts are new every day, as the Scripture says: *'Through the Lord's mercies we are not consumed, because His compassions fail not.* ***They are new every morning****'* (Lamentations 3:22, 23). He grants us good gifts according to our need.

If we know and trust our heavenly Father, we will learn, through the inner work of the Holy Spirit, to *'ask of God, who gives to all liberally and without reproach'* (James 1:5). We will ask, and we will receive; we will continue to ask more and receive more. We will then know and experience this unsearchable mystery that transforms our lives.

In sum:

- The Holy Spirit helps us know the Father

- He bears witness to our spirits that we are children of God
- He continues to remind our hearts that we are the children of God our Father, and that He is close to us and prepares good gifts for us

· The Holy Spirit also reveals to us the Lordship of Jesus

1 Corinthians 12:3 says, *'No one can say "Jesus is Lord" except by the Holy Spirit'* (NRSB). The Holy Spirit helps us to know Jesus as the Lord of our lives. The more He becomes Lord over our lives, the more we desire to do His will, and it becomes our delight.

Jesus does not take away our freedom. He only takes away the fake freedom that destroys us and instead grants us the true freedom that gives honour and preserves our dignity.[18] The Prodigal Son used his freedom in a way that destroyed him. When freedom is misused, it can be poisonous; therefore, we ought to let go of this poisonous aspect of freedom in order to be protected from the evil powers. There is a kind of freedom that the Bible describes as egoistic, earthly, sensual, and demonic (James 3:15). This kind of freedom causes us to fall into the traps of the enemy and be destroyed. The Holy Spirit asks us to leave behind this kind of freedom because it does not please Jesus, the Captain of our ship, whose Lordship liberates and frees us.

A master usually enslaves; however, Jesus is the only Master who liberates. A master usually dominates and crushes; however, Jesus is a Master who honours. Jesus said to His disciples: *'No longer do I call you servants ... but I have called you friends'* (John 15:15).

The Holy Spirit also helps us in allowing the grace of salvation to extend within us, and He reshapes our inner being to be conformed to the image of Christ (Romans 8:29). As a result of this

18 *'Therefore if the Son makes you free, you shall be free indeed'* (John 8:36).

process, Christ will be formed within us, each in a unique way. Christ's attributes are manifold; therefore, one may have joy, another peace, meekness, and so on. All these are Christ's attributes, and when Christ is formed within us, each one receives a different attribute of Christ. Consequently, we will appear royal, children of the King, princes and princesses, bearing the image of God—the image of His Son.

When Christ is formed within us, the world will see Jesus; thus, they will seek Him and love Him. We will no longer speak about Jesus using words that bear no life, but our message will be a living testimony seen and manifested in our lives and even on our faces.

Jesus is the only way through whom people can know God. Jesus said: *'I am the way, the truth, and the life. No one comes to the Father except through Me'* (John 14:6). It is also written: *'for there is no other name under heaven given among men by which we must be saved'* (Acts 4:12).

2. The Holy Spirit and the World

In 1 John 5:19 it says that *'the whole world lies under the sway of the wicked one'*. Though Christ has already conquered the devil, the execution of the full sentence of his defeat will occur on the Last Day. The devil cannot control the lives of those who know that he has been defeated, but he tries to deceive those who do not know this truth.

The devil is the ruler of this world. Jesus said: *'The ruler of this world is coming, and he has nothing in Me'* (John 14:30). If Christ is formed within us, we also can say the same words about ourselves. Though the devil is the ruler of this world and it is temporarily his, he has nothing in us as children of God. He has limitations in what he can do towards us. He has everything in the world, but not *the redeemed*—those *'with everlasting joy on their heads'*

(Isaiah 35:10). He cannot hinder them, because even the sea was parted before them and became a pathway so that they could cross over. He cannot sadden them because they have everlasting joy on their heads. It is a joy that casts away the distress and sorrow of the world. The redeemed are the salt of the world; wherever they go, they preserve and purify the place because the devil has no place in their lives, and the Holy Spirit occupies the whole inner land of their souls.

The Holy Spirit sanctifies us so that we may, in turn, sanctify the atmosphere around us, and the people may smell the sweet aroma of Christ instead of the odour of corruption and uncleanness that fills the world. This is our responsibility and the Kingdom work we ought to do. However, we cannot do anything on our own, as Jesus said: '*For without Me you can do nothing*' (John 15:5).

· The Holy Spirit is the One who sanctifies us and makes us holy

He is called *Holy*; therefore, the deeper our fellowship with Him and the more we give Him a place in our lives, the more He sanctifies us and sanctifies the world through us. As a result, we become holy, in turn becoming channels for the holiness of the world. People will thus see that our lives are pure and holy, not defiled or unclean with evil and lusts, and hence we will bear witness to them.

God granted us precious promises so that through these promises we may escape the corruption of the world and become partakers of the divine nature:

> *By which have been given to us exceedingly great and precious promises, that through these you may be partakers of the divine nature, having escaped the corruption that is in the world through lust* (2 Peter 1:4).

· The Holy Spirit is the divine fire that dwells in us

St. Macarius the Great (4th century) spoke about the Holy Spirit as fire, peace, and power.[19] St. Anthony the Great (4th century) also spoke about the Holy Spirit as fire. He told his spiritual children: *'Ask in uprightness of heart* ***for this fiery Spirit*** *and He will then be given to you ... Persist in prayer diligently, with all your heart, and He will be given you, for this Spirit dwells in upright hearts.'*[20]

He said these words to monks who already had an ever-growing fellowship with the Holy Spirit. Despite this, he said to them that they still needed something else; they needed *the divine fire.* This divine fire needs to be stirred and ignited. Apostle Paul said to his disciple Timothy: *'Stir up the gift of God which is in you'* (2 Timothy 1:6). He also wrote to the Thessalonians, saying: *'Do not quench the Spirit'* (1 Thessalonians 5:19).

The world around us is drowning in coldness to the point of freezing. God, the Holy Spirit, is fire. We ought to stir Him up and not quench Him. We need to be filled with God, the fire that warms and kindles the heart. St. Seraphim of Sarov (18th century) said:

'God is a fire that warms and kindles the heart and inward parts. Hence, if we feel in our hearts the cold which comes from the devil—for the devil is cold—let us call on the Lord. He will come to warm our hearts with perfect love, not only for Him but also for our neighbour, and the cold of him who hates the good will flee before the heat of His countenance.'[21]

Everything in the world seems dead, cold, and full of darkness. However, the children of God, the redeemed, who have the Holy Spirit in them as fire, find light amid darkness, warmth amid

---

19 St. Macarius, *Homily 9.25, The Fifty Spiritual Homilies of St. Macarius.*

20 St. Anthony, *Letter 1.38, Epistles of St. Anthony.*

21 St. Seraphim of Sarov, *On the Acquisition of the Holy Spirit.*

coldness, and power and victory amid the defeat that fills the world, because *'**He who is in** [**them**] is greater than he who is in the world'* (1 John 4:4).

The Holy Spirit, *who is in us,* is the pillar of cloud and the pillar of fire who went before the children of Israel and was light for them during the day and fire during the night. He was the pillar of cloud that overshadowed and covered them, and the pillar of fire that gave them light at night and protected them:

> *And the Lord went before them **by day in a pillar of cloud** to lead the way, and **by night in a pillar of fire** to give them light, so as to go by day and night* (Exodus 13:21).

Because the Holy Spirit is a pillar of fire, some saints, such as Seraphim of Sarov, were able to ascend the freezing mountains of Russia and pray there without feeling the cold. His disciples would wonder how he had not been cold. Then, looking at him, they would see his face full of light like a shining sun. He would tell them that the Holy Spirit in him gave him warmth; thus, he did not feel the cold that surrounded him.[22]

This enabled many hermits and monks who lived in the wilderness, wearing only one layer of clothes, not to suffer the cold nor the heat, because the Holy Spirit was their warmth in the cold and their breeze in the heat.

The Holy Spirit is tender; He is the Comforter. He refreshes our lives, brightens our ways, and shines upon our steps. He is the gift that has been granted to us, but the problem is that we do not know Him! Therefore, we need to know Him and enter into a true and deep fellowship with Him.

---

22 St. Seraphim of Sarov, *On the Acquisition of the Holy Spirit.*

3. The Holy Spirit and the Church

One of the old prayers of the Church says:

'O heavenly King, the Spirit of truth, the Comforter, who is everywhere and fills everybody; You are the treasure of goodness and giver of life. We ask You to graciously come and dwell within us, purify us from iniquity and save our souls.'

This means that the Holy Spirit is a Person, not only a power.

· The Holy Spirit comforts our hearts, alleviating fear, worries, and brokenness. He assures us, even regarding the future.

Therefore, Apostle Paul writes:

> *For **I am sure** that neither death nor life, nor angels nor rulers, nor things present nor **things to come**, nor powers, nor height nor depth, nor anything else in all creation, will be able to separate us from the love of God in Christ Jesus our Lord* (Romans 8:38, 39, ESV).

The Apostle is certain about the future: *'the things to come'*.

· The Holy Spirit transfers to us the life of Christ.

The Church is the Bride of Christ. When the Holy Spirit dwells in the Church with His power, work, and guidance, the Church of Christ will become as described in the Song of Solomon: *'Fair as the moon, clear as the sun, awesome as an army with banners'* (Song of Solomon 6:10). She will be filled with power, purity, and beauty. She will be glorious, *'having no spot or wrinkle or any such thing'* (Ephesians 5:27, NASB). She will have no sign of aging but will be full of life, beauty, and reverence.

- The Holy Spirit is the Person of the Trinity who prepares the Church as the bride of Christ so that Christ may come and find her ready and prepared for Him.

The Holy Spirit cultivates in the Church watchfulness and a life of continuous sanctification and purification, so that she may be ready for the coming of her Bridegroom, Jesus.

- The Holy Spirit connects us as one body and one family

> *For by one Spirit* ***we were all baptized into one body****—whether Jews or Greeks, whether slaves or free—and have all been made to drink into one Spirit* (1 Corinthians 12:13).

If we allow the Holy Spirit to work in our lives, He connects and unites us as one family—the family of God, or as the Scripture says, *'members of the household of God'* (Ephesians 2:19).

This unity does not happen by merely being friendly with one another, nor is it a connection on the social level. Rather, it is a special work of the Holy Spirit, who connects the hearts, and makes us members of the household of God. He inspires in us compassion towards one another, whereby if one suffers, the others would feel the pain, as the Scripture says: *'If one member suffers, all the members suffer with it'* (1 Corinthians 12:26). This kind of connection and unity cannot be described or even envisaged until we truly experience it as a true work of the Holy Spirit in our midst.

- The Holy Spirit transforms the parish into an actual house of God, where God is present, and the angels and saints are present

Even when the buildings of churches or monasteries are empty, their dust and stones are pleasant, because these places have been perfumed by the Holy Spirit. The Psalmist says: *'For Your servants*

take pleasure in her stones, and show favour to her dust' (Psalm 102:14).

- The Holy Spirit also brings life to the worship and ministry in the parish

He brings life to the prayers, liturgies, meetings, teaching, preaching, and any ministry conducted in the parish. When the Holy Spirit is present, everything will have a different flavour—the atmosphere will be different, and all the members will be one family—the household of God.

4. The Holy Spirit and the Individual Person

The Holy Spirit grants every believer the ability to perceive God's special plan and specific calling for his/her life.

He helps one to discover this plan, understand it, love it, and rejoice in it. The person will find in it the fulfilment of his ambitions and desires, whether the things that he thinks and dreams of, or even the things that do not cross his mind, but God knows them to be fulfilling for the person. When the person discovers this divine plan, he will find that he has all the talents and gifts necessary to carry it out. Moreover, he will receive the anointing of the Spirit for this specific calling.

The problem is that one sometimes makes a plan for his life—a plan of his own mind. It may be full of good ambitions, but the person may not have the gifts and talents needed to fulfil it. It may also be different from God's plan for this person's life. As a result, when the person begins to execute this plan, which he has made for himself, he becomes estranged from himself, becomes frustrated, and loses the way.

On the other hand, if one has true fellowship with the Holy Spirit and walks with Him day by day, the Holy Spirit will lead his steps, enlighten his mind, and help him discover God's plan and the things that God has prepared for him. The Scripture speaks about these things that God has prepared for those who love Him, saying:

> *Eye has not seen, nor ear heard, nor have entered into the heart of man* ***the things which God has prepared for those who love Him****. But* ***God has revealed them to us*** *through His Spirit* (1 Corinthians 2:9, 10).

We often think that this verse refers to the things that God has prepared for us in heaven. However, the verse actually refers to the things He has prepared for us here on earth because it continues on to say that *'God has revealed them to us through His Spirit'*. In heaven, there will be no need for revelations because we will be able to see everything clearly, face to face.[23]

If we allow the Holy Spirit to open our eyes to see and our ears to hear what our heavenly Father has prepared for us, it will be beyond anything we have ever seen or heard of. This is because God is love, and He prepares for His children things that are beyond their expectations or dreams. When the Holy Spirit reveals these things to us, we will find that they are better than our best dreams and higher than our highest ambitions. We will find that they truly satisfy our hearts, glorify God, and bless others. Thus, we will be blessed and will be a blessing (Genesis 12:2b).

5. The Holy Spirit and Ministry

The Holy Spirit is the divine power that works in ministry. He builds up the inner life of the servants of God, sanctifies them,

23 1 Corinthians 13:12

and makes them holy. He helps us fulfil the commandment that Apostle Paul mentions regarding ministers:

> *But in all things we commend ourselves as ministers of God: in much patience, in tribulations, in needs, in distresses, in stripes, in imprisonments, in tumults, in labours, in sleeplessness, in fastings; by purity, by knowledge, by longsuffering, by kindness, by the Holy Spirit, by sincere love, by the word of truth, by the power of God, by the armour of righteousness on the right hand and on the left, by honour and dishonour, by evil report and good report; as deceivers, and yet true; as unknown, and yet well known; as dying, and behold we live; as chastened, and yet not killed; as sorrowful, yet always rejoicing; as poor, yet making many rich; as having nothing, and yet possessing all things* (2 Corinthians 6:4–10).

· The Holy Spirit helps us to be *'ministers of the new covenant'*

The Scripture says that He *'made us sufficient as ministers of the new covenant'* (2 Corinthians 3:6). The ministry of the new covenant is a ministry of righteousness, grace, life, and glory (2 Corinthians 3:7–11). Therefore, those who carry this message ought to live accordingly, and their lives ought to reflect it. This, in turn, would allow the people we serve to get in touch with the Spirit of life.

· The Holy Spirit is the Spirit of Life

He raises those who are spiritually dead, comforts the distressed, and shows the way to the lost.

Through this work and companionship of the Holy Spirit, our ministry will be a living, fruitful, and blessed ministry that glorifies the name of God.

The Infilling of the Holy Spirit[24]

Readings

▪ Ephesians 5:15–21

See then that you walk circumspectly, not as fools but as wise, redeeming the time, because the days are evil. Therefore do not be unwise, but understand what the will of the Lord is. And do not be drunk with wine, in which is dissipation; but be filled with the Spirit, speaking to one another in psalms and hymns and spiritual songs, singing and making melody in your heart to the Lord, giving thanks always for all things to God the Father in the name of our Lord Jesus Christ, submitting to one another in the fear of God.

▪ Luke 11:9–13

So I say to you, ask, and it will be given to you; seek, and you will find; knock, and it will be opened to you. For everyone who asks receives, and he who seeks finds, and to him who knocks it will be opened. If a son asks for bread from any father among you, will he give him a stone? Or if he asks for a fish, will he give him a serpent instead of a fish? Or if he asks for an egg, will he offer him a scorpion? If you then, being evil, know how to give good gifts to your children, ***how much more will your heavenly Father give the Holy Spirit to those who ask Him****!*

24 This is a concise study about the infilling of the Holy Spirit that highlights some main themes. A more comprehensive study can be found in other books by the author, such as: the *Seasons of Salvation* series and *Men of God or Children of God* (Shine International Publications).

We have just outlined the indispensable work of the Holy Spirit in our lives and the great importance of being in fellowship with Him for the sake of growing in our personal spiritual life, our fellowship with God, our prayer life, overcoming the world, and our ministry. However, as the passage in Ephesians highlights, the Scripture commands us to be filled with the Spirit. Therefore, it is now necessary to explore how to be filled by the Spirit and how to remain in a continuous state of infilling.

The infilling of the Spirit requires three main steps:

- Emptying
- Surrender
- Trust

1. Emptying

If we want to fill a glass with water, this glass should first be empty in order to be filled. If it is already filled with something else, we can neither fill it with water nor keep water in it. Similarly, if we truly desire to be filled by the Spirit, we ought to empty a space in our inner being for this infilling.

However, we need to be honest with ourselves and search our hearts regarding whether we desire complete infilling of the Spirit or are satisfied with only receiving a small portion of the Spirit because we are not ready to go through this process of total emptying of our inner vessels. The more we empty ourselves, the more the infilling of the Spirit will be.

The infilling of the Spirit is a continuous process; it is not a one-off experience. According to the original Greek, the form of the verb *be filled* (Ephesians 5:18) indicates that the infilling ought to be continuous: we ought to continue to be filled again and again by the Spirit.[25]

Therefore, if we desire to receive a greater portion of this gift of God—the Holy Spirit—we need to empty ourselves completely so that He may flow in us abundantly, for the Scripture says: *'for God does not give the Spirit by measure'* (John 3:34).

The more the Spirit flows in us, the more we experience His deep, transforming work. We will also experience His companionship as a Person walking by our side, as the Psalmist says: *'He is at my right hand I shall not be moved'* (Psalm 16:8).

He also opens the doors for us and enlarges our path (Psalm 18:36), shining upon our steps.

He delivers our souls when we are cast down, restores our souls when we are low and frustrated, draws near to us when we are alone, heals us when we are hurt, and comforts us when we need help.

He is the Comforting Companion. He is the Lord, the Giver of Life. He revives us when we experience spiritual, emotional, or physical death. He overflows with His life that swallows up death and frightens the powers of darkness.

If we truly long to receive this precious gift of God—the Holy Spirit—we ought to be diligent in emptying ourselves completely from all hindering matters so that we may receive Him richly.

25 In the original Greek, the verb is in the present passive imperative. Paul wants believers to be filled continually, even moment by moment.

This process of emptying practically means a process of true and deep repentance.

We should examine ourselves to find the things that preoccupy us and occupy a big space in our hearts and minds. Examples of such things can be:

- Cares, entanglements, and material things

We should repent of these matters, remembering that the Scripture says: *'Casting all your care upon Him, for He cares for you'* (1 Peter 5:7).

- People who occupy much of our thinking and emotions, such as family members

Though we ought to love them, we should not be emotionally tied to them to the extent of allowing these emotional ties to overwhelm us and fill our inner beings. The Scripture says: *'Honour your father and your mother'* (Exodus 20:12); but, at the same time, it says: *'If anyone comes to Me and does not hate his father and mother, wife and children, brothers and sisters, yes, and his own life also, he cannot be My disciple'* (Luke 14:26).

This means that when our love for our mother, father, or relatives is fleshly and takes the utmost priority in our life, we need to repent and ask the Holy Spirit to help us to lay aside this kind of soulish love and grant us the true divine love for others.

- Soulish or emotional relationships and bonds are not limited to family members; they can also extend to emotional bonds with other people, including those of the opposite sex

This can occupy a big space within us and hinder us. We may discern that something is not quite right but may be unable to deal with it.

However, there is a significant difference between wanting to leave and lay aside yet being unable to, and not wanting to do so in the first place. In other words, in the first instance, we may truly want to get rid of a wrong emotional tie, yet might not know how to do so. In the second instance, we are not fully convinced that this tie is wrong or that we should get rid of it, and thus make compromises in order to avoid cutting it wholeheartedly.

If we compromise, it indicates that these relationships are a priority in our life. In such situations, we need to go to the Lord with trust and ask Him to free us from these incorrect bonds.

To sum up, total emptying is necessary in order to receive continuous infilling of the Spirit. Practically, to empty ourselves, we need to go before the Lord with a repentant spirit and allow the Holy Spirit to search us and see if there are concerns, entanglements, and preoccupations towards things or people. We should then ask His help to get rid of these wrong ties. Note here that it is important that we truly desire to get rid of them, even if we do not have the ability, because this will allow the Holy Spirit to come to our aid and enable us.

2. Surrender

Surrender means submitting to God's will and knowing that He has the upper hand and is in control of all things.

Our weaknesses can sometimes cause us trouble or problems. Also, when we open any door for the devil, the devil can find opportunities to interfere in our life. Despite this, we should know and have confidence that, above all our weaknesses, the devil, and circumstances, there is an upper mighty, fatherly, and faithful hand that controls everything.

If we sin, we ought to repent. But, at the same time, we ought to know that there is a mighty hand in which we can trust and rest assured. Even if our mistakes are what caused the trouble and problems we face, we ought to trust that, as long as we truly repent, God takes hold of all matters and corrects them. We should neither blame ourselves nor be complacent. Rather, we ought to maintain a healthy balance between having a true contrite and repentant spirit without the unhealthy guilt that can paralyse our repentance and inner transformation. At the same time, we ought to trust in the mighty hand of the Lord that corrects and redeems.

Therefore, we ought to trust that, even if the devil intervenes or takes control of a situation temporarily because we have opened the door for him, God will still make all matters work for our good as long as we repent. Consequently, what may seem a loss in the first instance will, in the end, become a gain. The story of Job is a well-known example in this context.

The Book of Job highlights how the devil may try to bring accusations against us. Sometimes, he is permitted to tempt or attack temporarily. As he attacks, he even tries to find opportunities to destroy—as he had tried to do with Job. As a result, the situation may seem dim and negative for some time. However, amid this darkness and difficulty, the divine hand remains in control, even if we fail to see it due to the dimness of the situation. Then, at a certain point, the divine hand is stretched out, correcting and restoring all that has been lost in a multiplied way.

In the end, we see how Job's possessions were replaced, how he was given children, and how his honour was restored. God *lifted up the face of Job* (Job 42:9) and instructed his friends—who had thought that Job was wrong—to go to Job to pray for them so that God might forgive them (Job 42:7, 8).

We need to learn to surrender, trust, and rest in God's faithful hand. As we walk with the Lord, we may pass through the valley of the shadow of death, the valley of humility and brokenness, the valley of fear, or the valley of loneliness and forsakenness; however, all these valleys are a divine training that will allow us to enter into new spiritual heights. It may seem as though we are handed over; however, the Scripture says: *'Though I walk through the valley of the shadow of death, I will fear no evil; for You are with me'* (Psalm 23:4).

This kind of surrender to the Lord allows the Holy Spirit to overflow within us and fill us. These infillings of the Spirit will be steadfast; they will never be lost or fade away.

Notice also that the commandment in Ephesians 5:18, which exhorts us to be filled with the Spirit, is followed by the following words:

> ***Giving thanks always for all things*** *to God the Father in the name of our Lord Jesus Christ* (Ephesians 5:20).

We may find it difficult to give thanks when we face difficult circumstances, dark times, problems resulting from our own mistakes, or attacks and reproach from the devil. However, in such situations, we must know that we are not forsaken, for God is our Father.

If we live a life of true repentance and are in constant living fellowship with God, the divine hand will be in control of every aspect of our lives. As a result, what seems dark today will shine brightly tomorrow, and what seems narrow and tight today will become broad tomorrow.

Surrender and giving thanks are two important aspects that open the door for the Holy Spirit to be ignited within us, work in our lives, and take control of all our matters. On the other hand, the lack of surrender and the lack of giving thanks grieve the Holy Spirit. As a result, we will not be in a state of continuous infilling and will consequently become weak.

Giving thanks is a sign that indicates that we have true inner surrender. We need to learn to thank God with a calm, peaceful heart amid difficult situations. This requires training. We need to patiently train ourselves to see and perceive the divine hand at work with us. If we look back and reflect on past events, we will find that we had frequently descended into various pits, or walked through different valleys, but always came out stronger than before.

If we put our full trust in the divine hand, we will not be afraid of the devil, circumstances, people, or even ourselves—our own weaknesses. Rather, putting our full trust in the Lord, we will say:

I will not be afraid of myself despite my weaknesses.

I will not be afraid of evil people who may come in my way—neither the Amalekites (Exodus 17) *nor the Canaanites, as the Bible calls them.*

I will not be afraid of the devil who may come at me with his cunning and deceitful plans or his traps and nets (James 4:7).

I will not be afraid of circumstances and unexpected things that may happen.

I will lift my eyes upwards from whence comes my help;[26] *thus, I will feel secure and be at peace.*

In this context, Apostle Paul says:

> *For I am persuaded that neither death nor life, nor angels nor principalities nor powers, nor things present nor things to come, nor height nor depth, nor any other created thing, shall be able*

26 Psalm 121:1

> *to separate us from the love of God which is in Christ Jesus our Lord* (Romans 8:38, 39).

The Apostle is certain regarding things to come because he fully trusts God, the *Pantocrator,* who is in control of everything.

This is the meaning of true surrender!

We should not ask God not to allow difficult circumstances, because we cannot direct God according to our own mind, we cannot see as He sees, and we do not know what is for our best as He knows. Difficult circumstances shape us and broaden us. It is written: *'Out of the eater came something to eat, and out of the strong came something sweet'* (Judges 14:14). This is a divine mystery.

Also, God is righteous, even with the devil. Therefore, if the devil finds an opportunity to attack at a moment when we slumber, God cannot prevent him. However, God will train us and help us to overcome and become spiritually stronger. The Psalmist says: '[He] *trains my hands for war, and my fingers for battle'* (Psalm 144:1).

Therefore, we should not focus on asking God to change circumstances, cast away the devil, and take away our weaknesses. Rather, we should give thanks, surrender, ask Him to teach us the lessons we need to learn, and ask Him to help us to grow through our weaknesses, distressing circumstances, and the battles of the enemy. We can still ask Him to cast away the devil and give us strength, but, the important point here is that we should not complain and grumble.

3. Trust

After emptying ourselves and training ourselves to surrender, we should ask for the gift of the Spirit because the heavenly Father says that He will give this gift to whoever asks of Him:

> *If you then, being evil, know how to give good gifts to your children, how much more will* ***your heavenly Father give the Holy Spirit to those who ask*** *Him!* (Luke 11:13).

Based on His promise and the commandment in Ephesians 5:18 to be filled by the Spirit, we should trust that we will be given what we ask for. Jesus also said: *'Ask, and it will be given to you'* (Luke 11:9). Therefore, He will surely give us if we ask.

The spiritual life is based on faith (2 Corinthians 5:7). Therefore, we should trust that if we have fulfilled the conditions and ask for the gift, it will surely be granted to us.

Three Main Channels through which the Holy Spirit flows:

- The Life of Prayer
- The Life of the Church
- The Life of Ministry

1. The Life of Prayer

The Fathers of the Church believed that the Holy Spirit Himself is prayer. Therefore, the more we have regular times of prayer and quiet times, the more the Holy Spirit will flow in us and continue to flow unceasingly. We will thus receive gift upon gift, infilling upon infilling, and power upon power. Therefore, having a regular and consistent prayer life is one of the essential channels through which the Spirit flows into our lives and fills us.

We also ought to learn to pray the Psalms, because when we are filled with the Word of God, this allows the Holy Spirit to flow in us. In the same passage that commands us to be filled by the Spirit, the Apostle continues, saying: *'Speaking to one another in psalms and hymns and spiritual songs, singing and making melody in your heart to the Lord'* (Ephesians 5:19).

When the Holy Spirit begins to fill us, we experience a profound transformation in our spiritual life. Our recurring spiritual problems, sins and weaknesses gradually fade away, and furthermore, we begin to receive the fruits of the Spirit, which grant us the opposite positive qualities and strengths. Additionally, the spiritual questions that had always perplexed us are resolved.

2. The Life of the Church

Church life, which includes repentance, confession, Holy Communion, and participating in the liturgical services and celebrations, is one of the channels for the infilling of the Spirit.[27]

Another aspect of church life is attending spiritual meetings and having fellowship with the brethren.[28] Fellowship is an important channel for the flow and outpouring of the Holy Spirit. As we attend the church meetings, we ought to feel that we are part of this family of God, hence being active members in the meetings, sharing in the singing and prayer, and listening to the spiritual teaching and messages.

3. The Life of Ministry

Apostle Paul says:

> *I am a debtor both to Greeks and to barbarians, both to wise and to unwise. So, as much as is in me, I am ready to preach the gospel to you who are in Rome also. For I am not ashamed of the gospel of Christ, for it is the power of God to salvation for everyone who believes, for the Jew first and also for the Greek* (Romans 1:14–16).

---

27 These aspects of the life of the Church are not inclusive, as we cannot fit all of them in the limited scope of this brief study. Refer to other books by the author (Shine International Publications) for more detail in this context.

28 Hebrews 10:24, 25

Also in Proverbs 11:25, we read: *'He who waters will also be watered himself'*.

We ought to have a holy burden towards the salvation of souls and proclaim to them the love of Jesus, the Saviour.[29] The more we care about others and their needs, the more the Holy Spirit flows in us. He waters us so that we may water others.

The more we water, the more we are watered. The more we give, the more will be given to us (Luke 6:38). This is a divine principle. According to material standards, when we give, we have less; however, in the spiritual world, when we give, we have more.

To sum up, there are *three conditions* and *three channels* to receive the infilling of the Spirit and continue to receive it unceasingly. The conditions or steps are *emptying, surrender,* and *trust.* The channels are the *life of prayer,* the *life of the Church,* and the *life of ministry.*

---

29 Romans 1:14–16

Part 2

CORRECT VISION OF MYSELF

In order to have a correct vision of ourselves, we should know our needs as well as our resources. We should also be familiar with our privileges as well as responsibilities; that is, knowing how to use our potentials and talents. Therefore, there are four main areas that we need to understand and be mindful of in order to have a correct vision of ourselves:

- Our needs
- Our resources
- Our privileges
- Our responsibilities in relation to our talents

The more one has a good understanding and correct vision of these four aspects, the more wholesome and mature he will be. From this, he will be able, through the guidance and inspiration of the Holy Spirit, to discover God's will for his life and fulfil it.

One of the major problems that believers face in their walk with Christ is living an inconsistent and unwholesome spiritual life. This kind of life leads to spiritual struggles and conflicts, which, in turn, cause the spiritual life to halt or regress. This happens due to having a frail and distorted personality or an unsanctified soul, as we will explain shortly. As a result, the person is unable to understand and discover God's will for his life and obey it. In some cases, the person may discover part of God's will but fail to obey it, and thus feel frustrated. In other cases, the person is unable to discover any part of this divine will, and hence moves unsteadily, not knowing which direction to go in. This spiritual state is the product of having a distorted, immature personality that is unable to see her needs, resources, privileges, and responsibilities.

When the soul matures and perceives correctly, it becomes a wholesome soul or personality, as Apostle Paul says in 1 Thessalonians 5:23:

> *Now may the God of peace Himself* ***sanctify*** *you completely; and may your whole spirit, soul, and body be preserved blameless at the coming of our Lord Jesus Christ.*

One of the meanings of *sanctification* in the New Testament is to be healthy and wholesome. The phrase *sanctify you* in this verse means to correct you and make you wholesome in spirit, soul, and body.

When the soul is not sanctified and wholesome, the personality will be distorted, barren, and frail. This practically manifests in being easily distracted and unable to concentrate or focus, having a great deal of fear, and not being able to discern right from wrong. Besides, the person is often confused, perplexed, frustrated, lacking the ability to be productive, and having extreme fluctuations between being enthusiastic about something at a certain time and losing this enthusiasm at other times.

All these manifestations indicate that the soul or the personality needs to go through the process of sanctification and correction, which is the work of the Holy Spirit within us. However, an important principle in this respect is that we do not just wait for God to work in us while we do nothing; we ought to be willing to go through the process of sanctification, and we need to complete the required preparation so that the Holy Spirit would accompany us and grace would be granted to us. There must be synergism between our will and role, and the work of the Holy Spirit.

However, if we are complacent and do not do our willful part, the work of the Holy Spirit in us will be hindered.

The hand of the Lord is stretched out to us, hoping and waiting for our hands to meet with His to work together. We may not know the way, but the divine hand will lead, guide, and direct us, showing us whether we should turn right or left, or stop for a while. Isaiah 30:21 says: *'Your ears shall hear a word behind you, saying, "This is the way, walk in it," whenever you turn to the right hand or whenever you turn to the left'*. It will be as if someone is speaking to me, guiding me and saying: *'This is the way; be careful, you took a wrong turn; there is danger ahead of you; the safe way is in this direction'*.

In 1 Corinthians 3:9, 10, Apostle Paul speaks of building the inner life: *'For we are God's fellow workers; you are God's field,* ***you are God's building****. According to the grace of God which was given to me, as a wise master builder I have laid the foundation, and another builds on it. But let each one take heed how he builds on it'*.

Thus, our soul is similar to a house,[30] having different areas or rooms. These inner rooms of the soul need to be opened and cleansed, and the damaged and distorted areas need to be corrected and healed through the work of God's grace. The more we open the rooms of our soul for the cleansing and sanctifying work of the Holy Spirit, the more God's grace will be outpoured into us, correcting and healing. If, for instance, a window is needed in one of the inner rooms of the soul, grace frames and fits this window. If a door is needed, grace fits a door and adds bolts to it so that sin and evil thoughts do not keep coming in and out, destroying us. When the required doors that prevent evil thoughts from coming in are missing, we end up being ruined and broken, and having a distorted personality. Though we may appear strong and pleasant to others, we may be in ruins internally. We might be laughing on the outside while weeping on the inside. We may be kind to people outwardly, yet harbour negative feelings toward them deep within.

---

30 Note that the New Testament uses three different metaphors to refer to the inner man: a house being built, a land that is sown, and a zygote that grows and is formed into a person.

A question may arise in this context: *'Does this mean we should tell people how we feel about them if we do not like them?'*

In fact, when the soul is corrected and sanctified, it acquires honesty and transparency, accompanied by sincere love. As a result, we can be frank with people without hurting them, because the truth we say is accompanied by love. However, if the personality is distorted and not sanctified, and the person tries to be open, the truth he says will come out as sharp arrows that may hurt the listener. We should neither be untruthful nor sharp and injurious. If we say something nice only outwardly, the recipient will sense a different reality in our soul, and what will be communicated to them is how we truly feel toward them.

When the Holy Spirit corrects and sanctifies the soul, pouring into it love and truth, we will be able to speak to others with purity, clarity, transparency, and truth because our soul will be pure and transparent. Our words will not hurt the recipient because we will be presenting truth mingled with love, which is healing, illuminating, and comfortable. Before the correction and sanctification of the soul, the truth can be mixed with soulish inclinations and motivations that are hurtful to others. It is therefore crucial to allow the Holy Spirit to sanctify the soul.

The sanctification of the body is an advanced spiritual stage. We read examples of it in the lives of the saints. The Holy Spirit sanctified their bodies to the extent that some were shining, some were elevated above the ground, and some were carried in the spirit from place to place.[31] They fasted and ate little without falling ill. Rather, they conquered illnesses.

When the Holy Spirit finishes His work of sanctification in the soul, He begins to sanctify the body. The body can reach a level of

31 This happened with Ezekiel and Philip (Ezekiel 8:3; Acts 8:39, 40).

sanctification where illnesses cannot conquer it,[32] and its natural needs, such as food and sleep, become no longer indispensable. The natural features change: illnesses and decay disappear. St. Macarius the Great, for instance, would sleep for only two hours per day, leaning on a wall, and this was sufficient rest for him.

Although these are advanced spiritual levels, they can be attained through the work of the Holy Spirit in any believer who understands them and desires to reach them. These graces are not limited to a select few but are meant for every person who desires to obey Christ and give Him an undivided heart.

In order to cooperate with the Holy Spirit, we need to understand and obey. The Scripture says:

> *My people are destroyed for* ***lack of knowledge*** (Hosea 4:6).
>
> *And I will give you shepherds according to My heart, who will feed you with knowledge and* ***understanding*** (Jeremiah 3:15).

Once we understand, we must choose to obey. Therefore, two issues need to be addressed in this respect: understanding and obeying. Often, these are the two challenges the human soul encounters: we either wish to obey but do not know what to do, or we know what to do but do not wish to obey. Thus, both understanding and obedience are necessary.

We can sum up this picture of the soul in two main points:

A. The human soul has become distorted due to the corruption of the fall and the fallen nature

When the soul is distorted and has not yet been sanctified, the conduct is often unwholesome, and we may thus act on the

---

32 St. Macarius the Alexandrian, for instance, lived for about 100 years without suffering from any illness, despite his strict ascetic lifestyle.

outside differently from our actual reality. At the same time, this distorted soul will not have doors or gates. Consequently, sin can freely enter, corrupting and destroying. Also, thoughts from the devil can come in, causing us to be angry or have unclean thoughts. We can thus feel that we lack the ability to reject sin and the devil and prevent them from entering our inner house.

In Matthew 12:43–45, Jesus likens the soul to a house, saying that, if the devil finds this house empty, he goes and brings with him other evil spirits and they come to dwell in this house; however, if he finds it occupied by the Holy Spirit, filled with grace, and adorned with spiritual ornaments, he cannot draw near.

We need to be honest with ourselves and examine whether our house has windows and doors, or if it is left exposed. The absence of windows indicates a lack of direction and being carried about by the wind. The wind comes in and carries us about to a certain direction. Then, the next day, the wind comes from the opposite direction and carries us in this opposite direction. Therefore, in Ephesians 4:14, Apostle Paul says: *'That we should no longer be children, tossed to and fro and carried about with every wind of doctrine.'*

However, if the windows[33] of our souls are closed, the winds of the enemy that blow upon the lands of our souls will not be able to get through or carry us about.

When the corrupt and poisoned winds of the enemy are directed to the relationships, they cause us to side with some people and reject others, and later perhaps reject those we had previously sided with. What kind of heart would this be—the heart that sides with people, rejects people, and seeks to please people?! This should not be the state of the hearts of those who follow the Lord. Apostle Paul says: *'For do I now persuade men, or God?*

33 The windows refer to the person's entrance points, meaning his senses.

Or do I seek to please men? For if I still pleased men, I would not be a bondservant of Christ' (Galatians 1:10).

When the winds are directed to ideologies, we may become enthusiastic about a certain idea and then reject it and become enthusiastic about another. For instance, we may at some point be enthusiastic about spiritual matters, sensing their great importance, then we may swing in the opposite direction, viewing them as extreme, and thus turn to earthly matters, such as focusing on outer appearance or status. This indicates that we have no defined direction, and cannot discern the precious from the vile, nor prioritise correctly. We fail to see that spiritual matters are not one aspect of life but are indeed the centre and lead of our life because Jesus is the only One who leads the soul to green pastures and still waters (Psalm 23:2). We are also unable to set our priorities right and to know that to everything there is a season.[34] God created the world in six days! Thus, we cannot do everything all at once but must discern the season for everything.

Therefore, one of the effects of the fall is that, when the windows of the inner house of the soul are missing, or perhaps one of its walls has fallen, the person feels as though his personality has no defined characteristics and his life has no defined direction. Consequently, people and circumstances often define his life.

Therefore, there is a need for inner sanctification of the soul.

When we come to the Lord, who alone can sanctify us, He shows us the divine image we were created in, which is unique to every person. God alone can correct our current, distorted image and restore it to the correct, eternal image we have been created in.

This is the true meaning of the correction and sanctification of the soul.

---

34 Ecclesiastes 3:1

B. Signs or manifestations of the sanctification of the soul

- The sanctified soul is filled with peace, and her conflicts disappear

Instead of the confusion, the distraction, and thinking of several things and wanting to do them all at once, light and clarity come to the person's mind, allowing him to prioritise correctly and discern the things he ought to focus on at a particular time versus the things he must postpone so as not get entangled with too many things and fail to complete any of them.

However, this act of sound prioritisation cannot be done only intellectually,[35] because one can think of a certain order and then, a few days later, he may change his mind about the order of priorities. But when the Holy Spirit sanctifies and corrects the soul, the person experiences illumination coming to his mind and peace overwhelming his soul. The light that comes to his mind helps him define his priorities. Previously, many matters would rush into his mind at the same time, and he wouldn't know or discern how to deal with them. However, after experiencing sanctification, one learns to wait for the right time for each matter, for there is a season and a suitable time for everything. Therefore, one should set his priorities correctly and not allow less important matters to encroach on these priorities. Initially, in the beginning, it may help if one writes down these priorities until they are established within him and he is no longer confused about them.

- Another sign of sanctification is that the emotions are cleansed and freed

Before this correction and sanctification, one has what we may describe as a sticky layer or coating on his emotions, causing him

35 Proverbs 3:5, 6

to either be attracted to people or repulsed by them. The passions dominate his life because he lives according to the flesh. Note that there is a difference between passions and desires. In Galatians 5:24, Apostle Paul says: *'And those who are Christ's have crucified the flesh with its **passions and desires**.'* The passions cause these attractions and repulsions. Therefore, if the emotions are not cleansed and sanctified, one's life will be an exhausting combination of attractions and repulsions.

The attractions enslave the person, and the repulsions cause him to lose his inner peace. Consequently, one loses his humanity and becomes a dummy.

Also, before this work of sanctification of the soul and emotions takes place, one can be emotionally sensitive and vulnerable, and may even become tense and uncomfortable if he senses that his feelings have not been considered, that he is not accepted, or that he has been taken advantage of.

Therefore, if the person desires to live a wholesome life in Christ, this process of correction and sanctification of the soul must take place. If it does not, his life will be filled with conflicts and will be superficial, weak, and frail, and he will suffer the consequences. He will not know what he ought to do and will be unable to live the fullness of the life in Christ which he is called to.

However, when the soul is sanctified, one's dealings and relationships will be wholesome and characterised by freedom. Scripture speaks about *'the glorious liberty of the children of God'* (Romans 8:21). This means that, when this liberty is complete, it is full of glory. It is not easy to describe this freedom which the Holy Spirit works in the emotions and in the soul, because the glory cannot be described; it can only be seen and tasted.

Scripture also speaks about the glorious joy—joy full of glory: *'Yet believing, you rejoice with joy inexpressible and full of glory'* (1 Peter 1:8b).

The work of the Holy Spirit in the soul and emotions leads to freedom from attractions, repulsions, and conflicts.

- **Another sign of sanctification is being rid of the spiritual paralysis and being able to obey the commandments with joy**

Sometimes, obeying the commandments is associated with experiences of failure; thus, we may dread this topic. For instance, we know from Scripture that we should love our enemies and turn the other cheek; yet we often find this to be difficult and may even consider it an advanced level that we cannot attain. However, when the Holy Spirit sanctifies and corrects the soul, He enables us and puts a girdle or a belt of power around our waist to strengthen us.

Additionally, we are often inclined to be slack and lazy, and sometimes even experience constant tiredness. In most cases, it is not physical tiredness, but rather a deep inner tiredness in our soul that cannot be resolved by sleep or leisure.

When the Holy Spirit corrects and sanctifies our souls, He girds our waist with truth,[36] straightening and strengthening our floppy and slack waist. We swing between self-pity and indifference because the waist of our soul is loose and floppy. It swings forward, pitying itself, and then swings backward with indifference. When the Holy Spirit performs His work of sanctification and correction within us, He puts on our waist a belt or a girdle[37] of power that

36 Ephesians 6:14
37 Luke 12:35

straightens and strengthens our waist, and hence we no longer swing forward nor backward but remain steadfast and balanced.

As a result, we will not pity ourselves when we are told a wounding word but will be girded and able to put the situation behind us without being hurt. This is because we will know that we have high, divine purposes, and that our dignity cannot be scratched by a mere negative word, because God bestows upon us great honour. In the same way, when we find ourselves inclined to sluggishness and slackness, the girdle on our waist will strengthen us to arise and perform our role, knowing that, when we willingly take one step, the Holy Spirit takes multiple steps to aid us; when we do but a little, He multiplies it.

God's blessings and divine gifts transform us deep within and change our outer circumstances. They restore us to being humans who are created for divine purposes, rather than dummies.

Now we move to the next section in this part about the correct vision of oneself:

Seeing One's Needs, Resources, Privileges, and Responsibilities

• Needs

The human soul needs *freedom, healing,* and *sanctification.* Freedom and healing are passive aspects, whereas sanctification is an active process.

The following are examples of things which may cause wounds to the human soul and from which it would consequently need to be healed and released:

- Past or recent experiences of hearing hurtful words from people, or going through difficult circumstances and suffering, may cause wounds or injuries in the soul.
- Recurring sins that continue for extended periods allow the devil to dominate certain areas in the soul, and hence these areas become paralysed. This, in turn, wounds the soul and requires sanctification and healing.
- Needs that have not been fulfilled during one's childhood and upbringing affect the soul and require dealing with. For example, a child needs to feel safe, secure, loved, appreciated, and accepted. If his parents fail to satisfy these needs, this child grows up with a distorted, wounded, and discontent soul, and would therefore need healing, release, and fulfilment of his needs.

These are the passive areas in relation to the needs of the soul.

However, the soul does not only need to be healed of her wounds, to be freed of her bonds, and to have her needs fulfilled. There is yet another important aspect: the soul must be transformed into the image of Christ.

The fallen human nature has acquired habits and characteristics that are not in agreement with the biblical picture of Christian life. These can be sleeping or eating habits, or any other unsuitable things that we get used to and become habits in our lives, and that we may not even notice. However, in the end, these are earthly habits of the Gentiles, not of the children of God. These habits ought to change and be replaced with the correct habits of God's Kingdom. We ought to measure our life against the standards of God's Kingdom outlined in Scripture, because we no longer belong to the earthly family in which we were brought up and which had its specific habits, nor do we belong to our friends who may have encouraged us to acquire certain habits; on the contrary, we belong to the Kingdom of God. Therefore, we must adapt to new habits and conduct that agree with the picture of God's Kingdom.

Scripture presents to us a clear example of how we ought to live on earth according to the standard of God's Kingdom through the Person of Christ who was incarnated, assuming human nature, and lived on earth with this human flesh in a particular manner, hence setting before us an example to follow.

Jesus is meek and lowly in heart.[38] We should be like Him. Therefore, if, for instance, we get angry when someone upsets us, we must repent and ask the help of the Holy Spirit to change this habit, allowing Him to sanctify our souls. We need to ask Him to help us change all the habits we acquired from our families, friends, and society, and instil in us new habits and a new nature.

We ought to search and examine ourselves and determine whether we have negative, hindering habits which we need to get rid of, and then learn the ways and customs of God's Kingdom to acquire them. We should set before us the example of Christ's life on earth. We should also look at the examples of the men and women of God who followed in His footsteps and lived as Christ lived. Scripture refers to them as *the great cloud of witnesses which surrounds us* (Hebrews 12:1). We need to look intently at this cloud and observe the various holy examples. As we do so, the Holy Spirit, who works in us to transform us, will portray to our minds the correct image that we ought to be transformed into.

The more we listen and respond to the Holy Spirit, the more He quickens our hearts and draws our attention to situations wherein we had behaved in a certain way but should have behaved

---

38 Matthew 11:29

differently. The Holy Spirit acts like a mirror, reflecting both our actual actions and the rightful actions we ought to have done.

Therefore, we must learn to quieten ourselves before the Lord and review our actions. In these quiet and sincere moments of reflection and revision in God's presence, the Holy Spirit draws near, helping us to see our actions and conduct that are unsuitable for the children of God and do not fit the picture of God's Kingdom. As a result, we realise our wrong actions. Then, the Holy Spirit would exhort us not to stop at the point of thinking that we were wrong and are bad, because this does not glorify God. Rather, we ought to focus on the picture of God's Kingdom which we need to acquire. The Holy Spirit would thus portray to our mind and heart the correct model conduct in such situations so that we may know it, remind ourselves of it, ask for it in prayer, and train ourselves to act according to it.

As we repeat this process of reviewing ourselves in God's presence, receiving the correct picture through the guidance of the Holy Spirit and the Word of God, and acting upon it, we are gradually skinned of our own fallen ways, and are transformed into the image of God's Kingdom, moving from one level to the other and from glory to glory. Thus, we receive grace after grace (John 1:16) and go from strength to strength (Psalm 84:7) until Christ is formed within us, as Apostle Paul says in Galatians 4:19.

It is a process of inner reshaping and transformation where the weak areas of the soul become strengthened, the distorted areas corrected, the proud areas humbled, and the areas that have the form of this world transformed.[39]

The soul is like a vessel into which grace is poured. The more this vessel is wholesome—not distorted, restricted, wounded,

39 Romans 12:2

or crushed—the more it will be filled with grace. It will broaden and be able to perceive the fullness of the will of God.

Our soul is also a mirror of ourselves. If half of this mirror is broken or blurred, we will only perceive a small part of God's will—half of what is granted to us. There will remain much more of what God has prepared for us, but we will be unable to see the fullness of it when half of our mirror is blurred, damaged, or broken. We can only see through the undamaged half. Therefore, the sanctification of the soul is a crucial matter.

· Resources

After perceiving our needs, we should also perceive the resources granted to us to enable us.

From the discussion about the *needs,* we understood that the soul needs freedom from the bonds of the evil one, healing from wounds and injuries caused by people or difficult circumstances, inner fulfilment, reshaping of our fallen habits and conduct, and transformation into the image of God's Kingdom.

How can all this be achieved?

This can be achieved through the *resources* that are granted to us to enable us to go through this process of transformation. These resources are: the Bible and the Church.

- The Bible

As we read the Bible, we should pray with what we read.

The Book of Psalms is a prayer book. The Pauline Epistles explain what Christ has done for us and the meaning of taking off the old and putting on the new man. We should read with this understanding and with a desire to apply what we read. For instance:

- The Epistle to the Philippians discusses, among other topics, joy and its manifold aspects. What are the practical steps to acquire this joy?
- The Epistle to the Thessalonians speaks about the second coming of Christ. How can we await His coming? It also speaks about faith, hope, and love. How can these be manifested in us?
- The Epistle to the Ephesians speaks about the Church, the Body of Christ. What is my understanding of the Church?
- The Epistle to the Colossians is about Christ, the Head. Do we truly see Christ as the Head of the Church?
- The Gospels speak about the Kingdom of God and the incarnate Christ.
- The Book of Acts reveals how the Church lived, grew, and extended by the power of the resurrection.

As we read, we begin to understand and perceive the correct pictures, notions, and steps that lead our lives towards spiritual growth and transformation into the image of Christ.

- The Church

The other resource is the Church. This is the practical aspect, or perhaps the workshop that helps us apply what we learn from the Bible. We can liken the Bible to lectures we listen to and learn at university, while the life of the Church and worship are like workshops, small groups, or laboratories where we experience the practical aspect of what we learn in the lectures.

The writings of the Fathers of the Church reveal to us how they understood the Word of God and how they applied it in their lives. Their lives present us with practical steps that help us and guide us in our spiritual walk.

If we fail to connect both aspects—the Word of God and its application—we will not progress in our spiritual walk.

Sometimes when we read the biography of a holy man/woman of God, we are deeply touched by it, yet we soon afterward forget it, dismissing it to be an advanced level impossible to achieve or be transformed into. However, the biographies of holy men of God are not meant to merely touch us. The Scripture says in Hebrews 13:7: *'Consider the outcome of their way of life, and* ***imitate their faith****'* (ESV). This means that we ought to look at their lives as examples that we desire to imitate, and long to be transformed as they were transformed, rather than just be touched by their biographies for a short while and then forget them.

Therefore, when we are touched and inspired by the life of a man of God, we should not stop there but rather think about how to imitate him. These men of God lived out the revelation and standards of the Bible. Thus, their lives are the practical application of Scripture; their lives reflect and illustrate the practical steps of the biblical verses. Thus, it is crucial to connect the Bible with the life of the Church.

Returning to the analogy of university lectures and workshops, if we only attend the lectures without practicing in the practical workshops or laboratories, we may struggle to understand some topics, and vice versa. We may acquire some theoretical knowledge, but lack the ability to apply it. Similarly, we should connect the Bible with the life of the Church. The Bible reveals the principles and the signs to follow, while the Church shows us practical examples of individuals who lived according to these principles and achieved their goals.

Additionally, the liturgical life of the Church is a channel of grace. The prayers, praises, liturgies, Psalms, doctrines, the faith passed down, and the examples of the Lord's servants are all considered channels of grace and spiritual aid on our journey of following Christ.

Therefore, the life of the Church is a channel of grace which enables us to receive transformative power.

To sum up, our resources are the Bible and the life of the Church. The principles and steps are outlined in the Bible. The practical application and channels of grace are in the Church.

· Privileges

Privileges refer to the blessings of redemption: '[He] *has blessed us with every spiritual blessing in the heavenly places in Christ'* (Ephesians 1:3).

God not only requests that we follow Him and be vigilant in our sanctification, but He has also granted us great privileges. He took what is ours and gave us what is His.[40] This is the true meaning of incarnation. All the acts that Jesus did in the flesh when He took our humanity became ours and have been granted to us.

Therefore, if we are in Christ, we are granted everything that He has done for our sake. For example, Christ ascended to the heavens; if we are in Him, this means we have also ascended in Him, as the Scripture says: *'Raised us up together, and made us sit together in the heavenly places in Christ Jesus'* (Ephesians 2:6). This means that our place of spiritual existence is not on earth, but in Christ. Thus, all enemies are under our feet. We must, however, acquire a correct vision and understanding to be able to enter into all that has been granted to us. We need to know that we are in Christ

40 *'For He was made man that we might be made God; and He manifested Himself by a body that we might receive the idea of the unseen Father; and He endured the insolence of men that we might inherit immortality. For while He Himself was in no way injured, being impassable and incorruptible and very Word and God, men who were suffering, and for whose sakes He endured all this, He maintained and preserved in His own impassibility'* (Athanasius, *On the Incarnation* 54.3).

and ought to live this out, meaning to continue to be in Him and not stray.

Another privilege that we need to view correctly is that, when Christ assumed our nature in His incarnation, He sanctified the body, and His holiness became ours. Therefore, we ought to view our bodies as holy and sanctified, not as vessels of lust and temptation. When Christ took on human flesh, He knew no sin; therefore, the flesh became sanctified.

If we fail to see and believe these privileges, they will not be active in our lives. But if we perceive them, and faith is stirred in our hearts, we will witness their results in our lives. For instance, if we understand what it means that He has *'made us sit together in the heavenly places'*, and our faith is stirred, we will be able to say: *'I am in Christ; therefore, the evil powers are under my feet.*[41] *I am in Christ; therefore, I will not be overcome by the world.*[42] *I am in Christ; therefore, the Father loves me and I am His. I am in Christ and Christ in me.*[43] *The heavenly Father is my Father.'*[44]

We receive these manifold blessings and privileges through Christ's redemptive work: His incarnation (including His nativity, circumcision, baptism, and temptations in the wilderness), crucifixion, resurrection, ascension, and sending forth of the Holy Spirit. The complete redemptive plan of Christ incorporates manifold blessings and privileges that have been granted to us. Let us look at some brief highlights:

The cross has conquered sin, death, and the devil. Resurrection has lifted us upwards so that we may be preoccupied with things above. To illustrate, it is like a child who has been afraid of a snake

41 Ephesians 1:20–23
42 John 16:33
43 John 17:21
44 1 John 3:1, 2

in his backyard. His older brother then kills it and tells him that it is now dead, yet he remains nonetheless afraid to even look at it. Thus, the older brother holds his hand and tells him to tread on it while holding onto him. Similarly, on the Cross, Christ put to death sin and death; by death, He trampled death. Then, in His resurrection, He told us that it was not enough to put to death all these things, but that He would also lift us above them so that we might seek those things which are above, meaning the heavenly matters: *'If then you were raised with Christ,* ***seek those things which are above,*** *where Christ is, sitting at the right hand of God'* (Colossians 3:1).

As for Christ's ascension, it grants us to dwell in the rest that Scripture refers to, saying:

> ***'There remains therefore a rest for the people of God.*** *For he who has entered His rest has himself also ceased from his works as God did from His. Let us therefore be diligent to enter that rest, lest anyone fall according to the same example of disobedience* (Hebrews 4:9–11).

Christ ascended and seated us with Him in the heavenly places. His ascension allows us to dwell in that rest and be filled with peace instead of our many fears. Our fallen human nature is full of different kinds of fear. We are afraid of ourselves: our weaknesses, lusts, and inner conflicts. We are afraid of not being loved by our parents. We are afraid of our friends, as some may be faithful while others may backbite. We are afraid of the devil and the future. We are even afraid of the spiritual life because we often fail to walk in it as we should; thus, we are sometimes frustrated or even become despondent. Christ knows that one of man's problems is fear. Thus, He did not leave us in this fear. He completed His redemptive work and seated us in the heavenly places as He knew that we would not be able to enjoy His complete work unless we were seated with Him. In the heavenly places, we are filled with comfort, rest, and trust in the fulfilling and tender Fatherhood of God that surrounds us and embraces us, in the divine love that compels us (2 Corinthians 5:14), and in the rich grace that comes after us. In our weakness, His power is made perfect because His grace is sufficient for us (2 Corinthians 12:9).

He surrounds us with the heavenly help of the angels whom He sends to serve us. Scripture says that the angels are *'ministering spirits sent forth to minister for those who will inherit salvation'* (Hebrews 1:14). We are also surrounded by a cloud of witnesses that overshadows us (Hebrews 12:1). The Holy Spirit dwells in us. We have the life of the Church and manifold channels of grace. He has granted us manifold graces of salvation, which we need to perceive, receive, and live by.

To sum up, the privileges are the blessings of redemption that have been granted to us through Christ, who became Man. He was incarnated, was crucified, arose, ascended, sat in the heavenly places, and sent to us the Holy Spirit.

If we have been granted such great privileges that set us free and lift us upwards to think of things above, we must realise that we have responsibilities as well, for privileges are always accompanied by responsibilities. This brings us to the next point:

· Responsibilities

Our responsibilities are related to putting our talents into action.

We have responsibility towards the Church, both the church we attend and the Church at large, as well as responsibility towards the world.

As for our responsibility towards the Church, we should be active members and faithfully use the talents God has granted us for our own spiritual growth, for the spiritual growth of our brethren, and for our church to carry out the fullness of her mission.

Each member is granted certain talents and gifts.[45] The more we recognise them and use them, the more spiritual energy will be added to our church; consequently, our church will be filled with manifold spiritual gifts and energies to serve and fulfil the needs of others.

There are other gifts and talents that we can use for the sake of the world. The circle of the world includes work colleagues, neighbours, and other people we may come across. What we offer our church differs from what we offer the world. Thus, our responsibility towards the Church differs from that towards the world. However, both circles fall within our sphere of responsibility.

In the Church, all the people love the Lord, worship Him, and serve Him. All members have the same faith, but not the same talents and gifts. Therefore, if a brother is cast down, I may be able to encourage him. Another day, I may be cast down or suffering from some kind of weakness, and my brother can encourage me. There may, however, be another brother who can help both my brother and me with a different matter that we cannot help each other with. This is the meaning of edifying one another, as we read in 1 Thessalonians 5:11: *'Comfort each other and **edify one another**'*. We also ought to *'stir up love and good works ... exhorting one another, and so much the more as* [we] *see the Day approaching'* (Hebrews 10:24, 25). Additionally, we ought to remind one another of the nearness of the Lord's second coming so that we may remain watchful and await Him with eager love.

However, with people outside the Church, we have a different mission. We should tell them about Jesus, who loves them and

45 Ephesians 2:10

has died for their sake to save them. We should tell them that though one may be spiritually lost like the Prodigal Son, he can be found. We should be light and salt[46] for them, illuminating their steps so that they may find the way, and adding salt to their lives so that they may overcome corruption and the loss of purpose. Consequently, they would be able to walk in *'the way, the truth, and the life'*.[47]

These are our responsibilities.

Finally, having a correct vision of ourselves means being able to see our needs, resources, privileges, and responsibilities.

---

46 Matthew 5:13, 14
47 John 14:6

Part 3

CORRECT VISION OF OUR ENEMY (THE DEVIL)

Readings

▪ 2 Corinthians 2:10, 11

Now whom you forgive anything, I also forgive. For if indeed I have forgiven anything, I have forgiven that one for your sakes in the presence of Christ, ***lest Satan should take advantage of us; for we are not ignorant of his devices.***

▪ 2 Corinthians 11:2, 3

For I am jealous for you with godly jealousy. For I have betrothed you to one husband, that I may present you as a chaste virgin to Christ. But I fear, lest somehow, ***as the serpent deceived Eve by his craftiness, so your minds may be corrupted from the simplicity that is in Christ.***

▪ 1 Peter 5:8

Be sober, be vigilant; because your adversary the devil walks about like a roaring lion, ***seeking whom he may devour. Resist him, steadfast in the faith,*** *knowing that the same sufferings are experienced by your brotherhood in the world.*

We will discuss this topic in two main points:

A. The schemes of the devil

B. How to resist and overcome the devil

A. The Schemes of the Devil

Before his fall, the devil was an archangel who had great power. In Isaiah 14:12, we read that he is called *'Lucifer, son of the morning'*. He is a cherub, which means that he is full of knowledge. Yet, he fell because of his pride and became the head of the evil powers. The Bible calls him *Satan, the serpent of old, tempter, roaring lion,* and *murderer,* among other names.

When this cherub fell, he became an enemy of God and of His purposes. God, however, does not have enmity towards anyone because He has no enmity in Him. He is patient and righteous, even towards the devil.

In His divine plan, God arranged to have two main dealings with the devil. The first was on the Cross, by which He disarmed the enemy's principalities,[48] defeated him, and broke his authority over humanity. The second will be on the Day of Judgement when the devil will be *'cast into the lake of fire and brimstone'* (Revelation 20:10).

During the period between the Cross and the Day of Judgement, God has granted the Church *'the authority to trample on serpents and scorpions, and over all the power of the enemy'* (Luke 10:19). He has granted the Church (and all her members, the believers) the authority to resist the devil and that he would flee from her (James 4:7). He has granted her the authority to overcome the enemy and be victorious.

---

48 Colossians 2:15

We often pray the words of the Psalm: *'Why do You stand afar off, O Lord? Why do You hide in times of trouble?'* (Psalm 10:1). We might cry out: *'Can't You see that the enemy is torturing us? Why are You forsaking us?'*

However, the truth is that God's ways are different from our ways. We expect God to deal with the enemy in our way. According to our fallen human ways, if someone upsets our friend, we get upset with that person for doing so. However, God is different. The devil is His enemy, and we are His children. Yet, when the devil wars against us, God does not strike him every time he attacks us. God has already struck him once on the Cross. He then expects us as His people to fulfil our role because He has given us the ability and authority to overcome the devil. This should make us aware that we are not little children. God does not want us to remain little children. He wants us to grow up. He has granted us His power and authority, saying:

Receive power from My Cross and My Blood to overcome.
Receive power from My Word and from prayer to overcome.
Receive grace and strength to overcome.
Satan is already a defeated enemy.

We ought to praise God for making us His offspring and granting us resources and weapons. We should therefore use these weapons.

Christ has already fought the main battle that we could not have fought, and He defeated Satan for our sake. However, now we need to trample on the devil ourselves and continue our walk. To illustrate, it is like a father who kills a snake outside his house that has been terrifying his child. He then tells his son that all the son would need to do after that would be to tread on it each time he goes outside. The father does not go out with his son each time to make him tread on the dead snake, because if he did so, the son would remain a child and would not mature. God wants us to be mature and not remain little children.

The first confrontation with Satan took place through the Person of Christ on the Cross. As highlighted earlier, God does not have enmity towards anyone, not even with the devil. As for the devil, his enmity is essentially directed towards humanity. Therefore, when God confronted the devil, this was done through the Person of Christ, who took our humanity. Through this first battle, Christ has shown us the path of victory and granted us the ability to be victorious.

In the final confrontation with the enemy that will take place on the Day of Judgement, God will judge humans, the devil, and all creatures according to His faithfulness, righteousness, and divine economy:

> *Then I saw a great white throne and Him who sat on it, from whose face the earth and the heaven fled away. And there was found no place for them. And I saw the dead, small and great, standing before God, and books were opened. And another book was opened, which is the Book of Life. And the dead were judged according to their works, by the things which were written in the books. The sea gave up the dead who were in it, and Death and Hades delivered up the dead who were in them. And they were judged, each one according to his works. Then Death and Hades were cast into the lake of fire. This is the second death. And anyone not found written in the Book of Life was cast into the lake of fire.* (Revelation 20:11–15).

God can never be unjust with the devil, even though the devil resisted Him; for God is righteous, upright, holy, pure, full of love, and His nature can never change. When the devil rebelled against God, God remained silent. Though the devil rejected God, this was not at all the reason behind the first confrontation between them. Rather, since the enmity is essentially between the devil and humanity, as soon as the God-Man came to earth, He confronted the serpent of old who wants to have dominion over the earth and desires to destroy the world and creation. Therefore, the first confrontation took place not because God had enmity with the devil but because the Perfect Man—the God-Man or the incarnate God—was on earth, and hence it was inevitable that He would face this power of the devil who wants to destroy humanity. At first, the devil tempted Christ, and Christ overcame.[49] Then, Christ confronted the devil on the Cross and defeated him and all his principalities, as Apostle Paul says:

> *Having disarmed principalities and powers, He made a public spectacle of them, triumphing over them in it* (Colossians 2:15).

These principalities and powers constitute some of the main ranks. When Satan fell, one-third of the angels fell with him. It was a whole camp of angels, perhaps millions of angels. When the Bible describes the number of the angels, they are described as *'ten thousand times ten thousand, and thousands of thousands'* (Revelation 5:11). This indicates that there are millions of angels. One third of them fell with Satan; therefore, the devil has a full camp of angels, among which are principalities, dominions, powers, and rulers, as mentioned in various books of Scripture.[50]

In the writings of the Fathers of the Church, we read about various evil powers that war against us, such as the evil powers of adultery, anger, worry, gluttony, laziness, sleep, vainglory, envy, and even the evil spirit of the bigger portion (meaning wanting to take the bigger portion when sharing anything with others). The spiritual insight of the Fathers of the Church was open and

---

49 Matthew 4:1–11

50 Ephesians 6:12; Colossians 1:16

they were able to see and discern the various kinds of evil powers which war against humanity. They were able to see *the spiritual hosts of wickedness* which roam in our sphere and battle against us.

On the Cross, Jesus broke the power of these different evil categories, defeated them, and disarmed them. Thus, the devil is now disarmed and he only relies on deceiving us, which is one of his main strategies.

Some of the main strategies of the devil:

- Deceit
- Confrontation and attack
- Threatening and blackmail
- Besiegement
- Envy

These are just some of the main strategies which we shall discuss below, but there are about ten or more strategies mentioned in Scripture. Each of them has its own dynamic. The more we understand the strategies and dynamics behind what the enemy does, the more watchful we will be. Apostle Peter says: *'Be sober, be vigilant; because your adversary the devil walks about like a roaring lion'* (1 Peter 5:8).

If we want to overcome the devil, we must be vigilant.

How can we be vigilant?

It is by knowing his war strategies, as nations do when they are at war.

1. Deceit

Deceit is one of the common strategies that the devil uses, for Scripture says: *'as the serpent* ***deceived*** *Eve by his craftiness'* (2

Corinthians 11:3). Scripture also calls him: *'Leviathan that **twisted serpent**'* (Isaiah 27:1) and *'**that serpent of old**, called the Devil and Satan, **who deceives** the whole world'* (Revelation 12:9).

He does not reveal himself outright but instead approaches the person in a concealed manner that appears good or beneficial on the surface, yet ultimately misleads the person.

He approaches us in a concealed and cunning manner, as he did with Adam and Eve in the form of a serpent. Since then, he has been employing the same tactic of disguise, taking on the appearance of various creatures. This creature can even be one's friend—a human being whom the devil uses to convey certain ideas that may lead one to deception. Who would ever think that one's friend could be a tool for the devil? It is difficult to conceive such a thought. Likewise, who could have imagined that the old serpent was the devil?

According to the Hebrew origin, the word *serpent* indicates a creature that glows or glitters. It was one of the most beautiful creatures. It was upright, standing on its legs. It was also the most intelligent creature; the Bible says: *'The serpent was more cunning than any beast of the field'* (Genesis 3:1).

Imagine Adam and Eve looking around and watching the animals and creatures in the Garden of Eden. As they were looking, they must have seen the cat, the dog, the mouse, the lion, and all the other creatures. The lion might have drawn their attention due to its strength and might, but the serpent must have impressed and allured them the most due to its beauty, glow, and intelligence.

Satan, the devil, must have been observing this scene and noticed that Adam and Eve had been impressed by the power of the lion and even more impressed by the glow of the serpent. Thus, he must have considered this and hence chosen to take the form of a serpent and a roaring lion.

As Adam walked in the Garden day after day, he must have admired the serpent, not knowing that it would soon be the cause of his fall. In fact, this deception by outer appearance happens in every generation; therefore, we ought to have open eyes and understanding. In 1 John 5:20, Scripture says: *'And we know that the Son of God has come and has given us an understanding, that we may know Him who is true; and we are in Him who is true, in His Son Jesus Christ.'* The Son of God has given us an understanding that we may know the truth. Also, Scripture says in John 8:32: *'And you shall know the truth, and the truth shall make you free.'* Our inner spiritual sight must be opened to see the truth and understand that not everything that glows is good. If we do not know the truth, we will not be free but enslaved to various things.

To sum up, deceit is one of the main strategies of the devil, which he can employ through a friend or a person who may appear gentle, nice, and tender. This is because the devil often comes in a cunning and concealed manner, appearing in various, alluring forms. Therefore, we need to be careful and watchful so as not to be deceived by the devices of the serpent. Moreover, our eyes must not be attracted to anything that seems alluring, but ought to examine everything because Christ has granted us understanding to know the truth, and this truth sets us free.

Scripture informs us that the devil often uses traps, nets, or a fishing hook with bait to ensnare us. This indicates that he allures us with what may appear harmless at first, but turns out to be a temptation, a trap, or a net. If we take the bait, we will be poisoned, for the bait hooks our minds and emotions, and paralyses our will.

These are the cunning and deceptive schemes of the serpent of old to tempt us.

2. Attack

Attack is another strategy the devil employs.

While *deceit* is one of his concealed strategies, *attack* is considered one of his manifest strategies, by which he directs his fiery arrows at us. In some cases, one may even feel as if the enemy is standing in his way, opposing him. In this case, it is not a matter of nice and sweet words of a friend or a gentle person, but a clear attack from the devil. It is a direct confrontation which can manifest itself in people being angry towards us, arguing with us, or speaking harshly to us.

The enemy directs his fiery arrows at us, causing deep inner wounds that may persist and remain painful for a long time. Healing from such wounds may take a substantial amount of time.

The Bible reveals this strategy of attack when it describes the devil as *a roaring lion* (1 Peter 5:8). The devil observed how Adam/man liked grandeur and power. Therefore, he often approaches people, especially the proud, as a roaring lion. For such individuals, he causes friction with others, confronting and attacking them in a direct way. Others may not be proud, but may be easily ensnared. For these individuals, the devil uses a fishing net or a trap. Some may not be watchful; hence, the enemy succeeds in placing traps along their path. Others may not be careful about what they see or hear; to them, the enemy presents bait, hooking them easily as they allow themselves to feed on uncleanness or whatever may come their way.

Others simply follow wherever their friends go, without discernment or caution about places they should avoid. Such people readily fall into the enemy's traps, and the devil employs this strategy against them.

However, those who are proud and deeply concerned with honour, status, and reputation require no subtle trap. For them, the enemy uses direct confrontation, stirring conflict and friction with others who may hurt them; then, he hooks them.

In conclusion, direct attacks are the enemy's strategy in which he directs his arrows at us, wounding our souls and leaving us half dead.

3. Threatening and blackmail

Another well-known strategy is the devil's constant buzzing in our minds and ears. He presents a thought to our mind and then persistently repeats: 'This situation is too difficult for you. You know yourself well; you are very weak and will not be able to do anything about it.'

He continues buzzing in such a manner, day after day and chapter after chapter, in the same story.

As a result, fear enters our heart, draining our faith and grace. As fear builds up and accumulates within us, faith and grace fade away, and hence we become more susceptible to easily falling into temptation. Then, the devil comes to us, saying:

'Didn't I tell you from the very beginning that you are weak and that the situation is bigger than you? You'd better keep this in mind and never forget it.'

These repetitive, negative thoughts, which the enemy throws into our minds and ears, become imprinted and stored in our memory. However, the enemy does not stop here; he keeps buzzing repeatedly, building up and developing chapter after chapter, hence filling us with fear, causing our faith and grace to fade away, and imprinting a certain negative impression onto our memories. After achieving this, the next time he employs this strategy, he only needs to knock on the door of our memories, reminding us that we are weak and that we will not be able to face the difficult situations and overcome them.

A well-known biblical story that highlights this matter is the story of Goliath, recorded in 1 Samuel 17. For several days, all Goliath did was put on his armour and cry out, reproaching the army of Israel and challenging them to find a brave man among them who could fight him. He terrified them with his spear, which was like a weaver's beam. He also intimidated them with his height. He puffed himself up, and the army of Israel became terrified. He spoke deceitfully, and they indeed were deceived. He continued to suggest to them that they had no man who could fight him. This reproach and defiance continued until David, the little boy, was anointed by Samuel.

God purposely chose David, who was described as small in stature, ruddy, with beautiful eyes, and of handsome appearance. This description signifies that he was not a tough person, but rather tender and delicate. He was a poet and a musician. Despite his tender nature, David's heart was strengthened by the Lord and set ablaze with the zeal of the Lord. Thus, he said:

> *For who is this uncircumcised Philistine, that he should defy the armies of the living God?* (1 Samuel 17:26).

Then, he said to Goliath:

> *You come to me with a sword, with a spear, and with a javelin. But I come to you* ***in the name of the Lord of hosts,*** *the God of the armies of Israel, whom you have defied* (1 Samuel 17:45).

When Goliath saw David, he disdained him and said:

> *Am I a dog, that you come to me with sticks?* (1 Samuel 17:43).

For David, a sling and a stick were sufficient to make this giant fall, and then he killed him with his own sword.

The important principle here is that the threat of the devil can be overcome by faith and the Word of God.

Therefore, when the enemy approaches us, buzzing in our ears and minds with the thought that we will surely be defeated and taken captive, we must proclaim the Word of God. This proclamation is similar to pointing the sling and the stick at the enemy to make him fall. Examples of these proclamations are the words of Scripture that say:

- *Let the weak say, 'I am strong'* (Joel 3:10).
- *He will not allow your foot to be moved* (Psalm 121:3).
- *He who keeps* [me] *will not slumber. Behold, He who keeps Israel shall neither slumber nor sleep. The Lord is* [my] *keeper; the Lord is* [my] *shade at* [my] *right hand. The sun shall not strike* [me] *by day, nor the moon by night. The Lord shall preserve* [me] *from all evil'* (Psalm 121:3b–7a).

We should proclaim these verses with might, holding the stick and *'the sword of the Spirit, which is the word of God'* (Ephesians 6:17), in the face of the enemy.

As a result, the devil, who continuously buzzes in our ears, will be terrified and withdraw. He will be weakened and fall, knowing that there is a God in Israel. After that, we should take the sword of the enemy and cut him up, declaring that all his threats are false and are lies.

We ought not only to defeat the enemy, but we must then pursue him and destroy him, as the Psalmist says:

> *I have **pursued my enemies** and overtaken them; neither did I turn back again **till they were destroyed*** (Psalm 18:37).

We ought to pursue the enemy and destroy him so that he may not threaten other people. We should go after him with his own sword, meaning his own way and strategy, which he has been using with us. As he has been buzzing relentlessly in our minds, saying: 'Haven't I told you that you are weak and will not be able to overcome?', we will also pursue him, saying to him: 'Haven't we told you that you are a liar and that all your threats are false?'

When the enemy attacks and threatens, he desires to murder. The Scripture describes him thus, saying:

> *He was a murderer from the beginning, and does not stand in the truth, because there is no truth in him. When he speaks a lie, he speaks from his own resources, for he is a liar and the father of it* (John 8:44).

He desires to destroy the person if he can, leaving him half dead. However, God has granted us all the necessary weapons and armour to overcome the devil.

The devil is also a roaring lion. On the other hand, the Scriptures speak of Christ as the Lion of the tribe of Judah[51] who has prevailed. He has confronted this other lion, the devil, and has broken his teeth.[52] Therefore, Satan is a lion with broken teeth. He can only make a sound, a roar. He acts out by making loud noises and roaring. But we should be aware that he cannot bite, as he has no teeth; he only lets out empty roars.

4. Besiegement

Scripture speaks about the nets of the enemy.

One of the strategies of the enemy is to throw invisible nets over people. When we try to come out of such a net, we find ourselves

51 Revelation 5:5
52 Psalm 3:7

besieged from all directions. We experience this state when we go through various circumstances that tighten around us from every direction, causing us to feel distressed and pressured.

The devil employed this strategy with Israel of old by causing their enemies to lay siege around Jerusalem until the Israelites completely ran out of food and starved, and even causing their enemies to cover their wells to ensure they would thirst to death.

The enemy still uses this method on us as well. He besieges us in various ways. As a result, as we pray the Psalms, for instance, we may find ourselves distracted and unable to understand the words. Then, even as we keep trying to concentrate and continue the prayer, we may find ourselves constantly distracted by the issue or problem we are facing at that time. We may then give up and decide to try again the next day. However, the same thing happens again the next day, and it continues for several days, which causes the spiritual food and the living water to run out. In such a state, we are in a spiritual siege. Continuing in this state leads to spiritual death.

We must stay watchful in such situations and pray the words of the Psalm: *'Pull me out of the net which they have secretly laid for me'* (Psalm 31:4). If, despite this, we still fail to get out of the net, we should seek the help of our spiritual guide and brethren. As a result, the hand of the enemy, which had laid this net, will be broken, the net will fall off, and we can then escape.

5. Envy

The devil envies humanity because of the divine love and rich grace that is continually granted to us in Jesus Christ. However, in order for the devil to direct his envy towards us, he must find a gap. How does he find this gap?

It is a simple matter which often happens in our lives, but which we do not notice.

For example, we might suffer from a recurring sin and desire to get rid of it. Then, at some point, we notice that we hadn't fallen into this sin for two or three weeks. Thus, a thought may come to our mind, saying, 'Oh, it has been three weeks, and I haven't fallen into this sin that I'm used to committing three times a week. I should thank God for this.' What often happens is that the next day, we find that we fall into this sin again. We will thus be surprised because we had just been rejoicing the prior day that we had overcome this sin. Hence, we will begin to wonder if we have fallen into pride because of our success, or will wonder what is happening.

Why does this happen, and what does it mean?

When we overcome anger, for example, and go a whole month without getting angry, this indicates that we have received a special grace. When the devil sees this, he envies us for this grace and desires to find a gap to enter and snatch it from us. Thus, he knocks, hoping we will open a gap through which he can enter. He tells us, 'The grace that you received is great. Shouldn't you thank God for it?' Consequently, we would think it is truly wonderful to have stopped this sin and to have received this grace. As soon as we open the window, the hand of the devil comes in and snatches the grace from us. When one considers that it is wonderful to have stopped this sin and received this grace, it may lead to pride or a lack of vigilance in establishing and guarding the grace received; therefore, it opens the door for the enemy to steal or snatch this grace from him.

Therefore, when we notice a grace in our life, we should not only thank God but also confess that this is His grace, and ask God that it may be kept and preserved within us. We should ask Him to strengthen us in our weakness and help us to be vigilant. We should then continue to watch, be vigilant, and be careful until this grace is confirmed more and more within us.

We should also continue to long for grace after grace.[53] We should not only stop being angry, but should also strive to be meek and pure, not only seeking one grace but manifold graces.[54] We should continue to be watchful over the grace we receive until we are steadfast in it.

This is the level of spiritual watchfulness required in order to overcome the envy of the devil.

---

53 John 1:16
54 1 Peter 4:10

B. How to Overcome the Devil

Readings

▪ **James 4:7, 8**

Therefore submit to God. ***Resist the devil and he will flee from you.*** *Draw near to God and He will draw near to you. Cleanse your hands, you sinners; and purify your hearts, you double-minded.*

▪ **Revelation 12:10, 11**

Then I heard a loud voice saying in heaven, "Now salvation, and strength, and the Kingdom of our God, and the power of His Christ have come, for the accuser of our brethren, who accused them before our God day and night, has been cast down. And ***they overcame him by the blood of the Lamb and by the word of their testimony, and they did not love their lives to the death****.*

Overcoming the devil requires three essential resources:

- The Power of Redemption
- The Word of God
- Spiritual Weapons

Scripture highlights other things that can help us overcome the devil, but they can be included under these three main headings.

Scripture teaches us to resist the devil, assuring us that when we resist him, he will flee from us.

How can we resist the devil?

By using the previously mentioned resources.

As a foundational principle in spiritual life, when Scripture states a certain truth, this indicates that it is practically possible to live it out. Therefore, when Scripture exhorts us to resist the devil, this indicates that this act is within the ability of every person; it also indicates that the devil will indeed flee from us if we resist him.

God is the highest King over both the visible kingdoms of the earth and the invisible kingdoms, among which is the kingdom of darkness. He is the ruler over the Kingdom of light (His children), the kingdom of darkness (of the devil), and the kingdoms of the earth. In Revelation 1:5, we read that Jesus Christ is *'the ruler over the kings of the earth.'* Because God is righteous and just, even the devil, who always opposes God, submits to the precepts and judgements of God. Since there are no gaps or flaws in these precepts and judgements, the devil cannot contradict them nor bring charges or accusations against them. However, the devil constantly tries to take advantage of these precepts and use them against the children of God, especially against those of the children of God who are ignorant of God's laws and statutes. Due to our ignorance of God's statutes, the devil succeeds in deceiving us.

For example, one of these divine laws and precepts is that God does not allow us to be tempted beyond what we are able, as the Scripture states in 1 Corinthians 10:13:

> *No temptation has overtaken you except such as is common to man; but God is faithful, who will not allow you to be tempted beyond what you are able, but with the temptation will also make the way of escape, that you may be able to bear it.*

Who is the tempter?

Apostle James clarifies this matter by saying:

> *God cannot be tempted by evil, nor does He Himself tempt anyone. But each one is tempted when he is drawn away by his own desires and enticed* (James 1:13, 14).

The devil is behind the temptations. He is called *the tempter,* as Apostle Paul highlights in his Epistle to the Thessalonians: *'lest by some means* ***the tempter*** *had tempted you, and our labour might be in vain'* (1 Thessalonians 3:5).

What is a temptation?

A temptation is a challenge or difficulty, possibly caused by certain circumstances that one goes through.

Who is behind these circumstances?

The powers of darkness are behind them.

However, there is a biblical principle that we will never have to face a power or a rank of the kingdom of darkness beyond our ability to resist. Therefore, God will not allow any of His children whose spiritual stature is one meter, for example, to be confronted by an evil power that is three meters tall. In Genesis 6, we read about the giants on earth. We also read about Goliath who was over 3 meters tall. This means that there are powerful ranks in the kingdom of darkness, who, if described in our material language, would be considered the giants of the earth. These giants confronted God's people in the Old Testament during various eras. High ranks of the powers of darkness operated through them.

The devil wants to constantly destroy. However, God has laws and rules that have to be followed and implemented.

Who is responsible for ensuring that these laws are followed and implemented?

On earth, this is the responsibility of Christ's Church. In heaven, it is the responsibility of the angels.[55]

Based on this understanding, if one of God's children is about to face a strong power of darkness bigger than him, the angels will immediately confront this power and push it away, asserting that it has no right to confront this person, as there are rules in place. The rule that governs this matter is that no one will be tempted beyond his ability; thus, this strong evil power has no right to confront this little child of God; therefore, the angels will push it away.

If our spiritual insight were open, we would be able to see that many temptations never reach us because the angels face them and finish these battles before they reach us.

All these matters submit to the laws of God's Kingdom and the righteousness of God, the King. He is *'righteous in all His ways, and* [merciful] *in all His works'* (Psalm 145:17). He is fair and just with His children and with the devil, and He will continue to be so until the Day of Judgement, when everyone, both humans and the devil, will be judged according to God's faithfulness and righteousness, and according to His laws.

Returning to the promise that we will never face a power bigger than us, we ought to be reassured that we always have the ability to overcome when we are tempted. Therefore, we should keep the following three principles in our minds:

- We will never be confronted by an evil power bigger than us
- If an evil power confronts or attacks us, it is within our spiritual ability to overcome it by using the resources granted

55 The angels always fulfil their roles and duties, but it is important that we are also watchful and fulfil our role!

to us, because it will never be bigger than us, and because Scripture says that if we resist the devil, he will flee from us

- Therefore, if for some reason, we are overcome by an evil power that attacks us, this indicates a certain shortcoming on our part. This can be due to one of the following two reasons:
    - A lack of knowledge and understanding of the divine principles, the strategies of the devil, the spiritual weapons, and the resources granted to us
    - A lack of faithfulness whereby, despite knowing all these principles and resources, we are not vigilant in obeying and following what we know

After understanding the three main principles, we now need to learn the three main resources that help us overcome the devil:

- The Power of Redemption
- The Word of God
- Spiritual Weapons

1. The Power of Redemption

This refers to all of Christ's acts that He completed for our redemption, because all that Christ has done for our sake essentially aims at freeing and releasing us from the devil and his destructive work by which he distorts the human personality.

When Satan deceived Adam, and Adam fell, this resulted in slavery (Satan enslaved man) and inner corruption, which entered human nature.

Therefore, in His redemption, Christ reversed the effects of the fall. The cross provides us with the weapons to overcome the devil and the ability to deal with the inner corruption through sanctification.

In fact, all the acts of salvation and redemption are resources given to us to overcome the devil and the effects of the fall.

Our problem is that we are either ignorant of the resources granted to us, or we see only one resource, focus on it alone, and forget the others. In fact, each resource has its own value and role in our life. The more familiar we are with the diversity of our resources, the more we will be able to overcome all kinds of temptations and trials.

A brief word about each of these resources or tools:

- *The blood of Jesus is a powerful tool against the devil*

In the Book of Revelation, we read: *'And they **overcame him by the blood of the Lamb** and by the word of their testimony'* (Revelation 12:11).

- *The Cross*

In the Epistle to the Colossians, we read: *'Having disarmed principalities and powers, He made a public spectacle of them, triumphing over them in it* [the Cross]*'* (Colossians 2:15).

Therefore, the blood of Jesus and His Cross grant us victory over the enemy, as they terrify the powers of darkness.

The Early Church Fathers held a cross while praying, and they often crossed themselves.[56] They resisted the enemy and overcame him by the Cross. The Cross is the sign of victory.

Since man has a spirit and a body, all spiritual matters have a faith aspect and a mystical aspect. Therefore, we need to see all the resources given to us holistically, that is, to see their faith aspect and mystical aspect, the inner and outer, the spiritual and material.

The faith aspect about the blood of Jesus is related to what Scripture reveals about it. The more we understand, pray, and exercise our faith, the more we receive its work and power in our lives. We should also not forget about the mystical aspect, which is the body and blood of Jesus that we receive in holy communion, because Christ Himself established this mystery.

The same applies to the Cross. The more we understand the work of the Cross as revealed in Scripture, pray about it, and seek it, the more we receive its work and power in our lives. Also, when we hold a cross and cross ourselves as we pray, as the Early Church

---

56 '*Early Church Fathers like Tertullian (c. AD 155–220) urged Christian believers to build the simple but meaningful sign of the cross into their everyday experience. He wrote:* "At every forward step and movement, at every going in and out, when we put on our clothes and shoes, when we bathe, when we sit at the table, when we light the lamps, on the couch, on a seat, in all the ordinary actions of daily life, we trace upon the forehead the sign" *(Tertullian of Carthage, De Corona, in Ante-Nicene Fathers, eds. Alexander Roberts, James Donaldson, and A. Cleveland Coxe, trans. S. Thelwall (Buffalo: Christian Literature Publishing Co., 1885), 3:193.)*

A century later, Cyril of Jerusalem (AD 313–386) shared a similar view: "Let us, therefore, not be ashamed of the Cross of Christ ... seal it upon thy forehead, that the devils may behold the royal sign and flee trembling far away. Make this sign at eating and drinking, at sitting, at lying down, at rising up, at speaking, and at walking. In a word, at every act" *(Cyril of Jerusalem, "Catechetical Lecture IV: On the Tens Points of Doctrine," in vol. 7, Nicene and Post-Nicene Fathers, Second Series, eds. Philip Schaff and Henry Wace, trans. Edwin Hamilton Gifford (Buffalo: Christian Literature Publishing Co., 1894), 135).*

The sign of the cross was a public profession of faith in the Crucified One. It declared to both the world and the devils that this person was marked as Christ's own.'

(Elmer, Robert. "Why Do Some Christians Make the Sign of the Cross—& Others Don't?" *Word by Word*, 14 Apr. 2023, www.logos.com/grow/nook-christians-sign-of-the-cross/.)

Fathers did, we open the way for the mystical aspect, hence mystically receiving the work and power of the cross.

This is because, as highlighted earlier, man is both a spirit and a body. We communicate with the visible, material world and the invisible, spiritual world. We deal with the powers of darkness as spirits, but also in evil people through whom these spirits operate. Therefore, we cannot focus on only one aspect and ignore the other. The beauty of the teaching of the Church is that it helps us see a complete picture, and not focus only on one aspect and neglect the other.

- ***The Resurrection of Christ is another resource in overcoming the devil***

In the Cross, the devil has been defeated, and in the resurrection, the victory has been proclaimed.

As the Church continues to celebrate the resurrection during the Holy Fifty (the fifty days from Easter to Pentecost) through liturgical worship and joyful hymns, these outer celebrations speak to our visible aspect, igniting our faith. As a result, our faith increases and grows, and our whole being becomes filled with the power of resurrection, as the Apostle says: *'That I may know Him and the power of His resurrection'* (Philippians 3:10).

The more the power of resurrection fills our inner being, the more the devil will be terrified to come near us.

Therefore, as mentioned earlier, it is important to perceive the resources that are granted to us to resist the enemy—to perceive them in their full broadness, and not only focus on one aspect and neglect the other. We ought to see both the faith aspect and the mystical aspect—the aspect revealed in the Word of God, and the mystical aspect lived and practised in our own daily life and manifested in the Church's celebrations of the seasons of salvation. As a result, our whole being can receive and experience the divine work.

Redemption is offered to our whole being. There is even redemption for the body, which will reach its fullness when we put on the glorious bodies. However, there can be some early manifestations of it now. The Church Fathers experienced a foretaste of the manifestation of redemption in their bodies. They experienced lightness in their bodies, being carried in the spirit from place to place,[57] light radiating from their faces and fingers during prayer at times, and haloes appearing around their faces. These are all examples of early manifestations of the redemption of the body while they were still living in the flesh.

- *The Ascension of Christ is another resource in overcoming the devil*

When Christ ascended, He seated us with Him *'above all principality and power and might and dominion'* (Ephesians 1:21). Through this salvific act of Christ, we can overcome the devil and proclaim that he is under our feet.

However, we cannot proclaim this divine truth without understanding its true meaning; otherwise, they will be mere words that bear no power and thus the devil will mock us and overcome us. We may have already experienced repeating these phrases without reaping any results or overcoming the devil. The reason is that we do not understand them, nor do we perceive the divine truth that would allow us to exercise our faith.

In order to confront the devil and tell him that he is under our feet, we must understand what happened in Christ's ascension. When

57 Refer to the biblical examples of Philip (Acts 8:39) and of Ezekiel (Ezekiel 8:3).

Christ ascended, He lifted us up with Him and seated us with Him. Since Christ is seated above all the ranks of the powers of darkness, our place in Him is above all these ranks—*'all principality and power and might and dominion'* (Ephesians 1:21); therefore, they are also under our feet, inasmuch as we are established in Him.[58]

After Christ ascended, He sent to us the Promise of the Father on the Day of Pentecost.

- ***The Holy Spirit is another resource that helps us overcome the devil***

In Isaiah 59:19, we read:

> *When the enemy comes in like a flood, the Spirit of the Lord will lift up a standard against him.*

In other translations, the last phrase reads: *'driven on by the breath of the Lord'* (NABRE), or *'which the breath of the Lord drives'* (AMP).

Therefore, we notice that many of the Church Fathers, both in ancient and modern history, would breathe or blow into the person when casting out demons from him, and the demon would indeed be driven away. This is because of the breath of the Holy Spirit who dwelt in them. They would also use the cross and the sign of the cross in casting out demons, for these are true resources granted to us to overcome the enemy.

We mentioned earlier that the devil has different strategies, and that sometimes he comes in a hidden way, while at other times, he attacks openly and directly.

The spiritual resource that we use to overcome the enemy depends on how he comes to us. From the verse above, we understand

---

58 John 14:20; 1 Corinthians 12:13

that sometimes he comes as a flood. This is a direct attack. In this case, our weapon to overcome him would be the Spirit of God, as the verse states. Practically, this direct attack of coming like a flood could be an onslaught of evil and overwhelming thoughts, suggesting to us that there is no hope, that we are defeated, and that we should not even try. When this happens, we ought to proclaim: *'The breath of the Lord will drive you away.'*

Unfortunately, what often happens is that we repeat such proclamations as mere phrases that are void of power due to our lack of understanding of the resources available to us and our lack of understanding of how to confront the enemy. As a result, we fail to be victorious in our spiritual battles and confrontations with the enemy, despite being granted this victory in Christ!

To sum up, the power of redemption as a tool to overcome the enemy includes the blood of Jesus, the cross, the resurrection, the ascension, and the power of the Holy Spirit.

2. The Word of God

The Word of God is another resource or tool that we can use to overcome the devil. In Ephesians 6:17, we read that the sword of the Spirit is the Word of God. Also, when Satan tempted Jesus in the wilderness (Matthew 4 and Luke 4), Jesus overcame him by the Word of God. He could have used other means, yet in this confrontation He chose to overcome by the Word of God. At that time, the blood of sacrifices was already being used as a shadow and symbol of the blood of Jesus. Also, in the divine economy, the blood of Jesus has been shed before the foundation of the world (Revelation 13:8). Therefore, this tool was available for Christ; however, in this temptation, He answered Satan using the Word of God. On other occasions, we see Jesus using other tools in overcoming the devil. For instance, He cast out demons with a word, as we read in Matthew 8:16. In this case, He used the power of redemption. He is the Redeemer of humanity, and so He ordered the demons to come out using a word.

Sometimes, the devil himself tries to deceive us by misusing the Word of God. For example, he may say to us: *'Isn't it written: "Render therefore to Caesar the things that are Caesar's, and to God the things that are God's"?*[59] *Don't take extremes; you ought to be a balanced person. Why won't you give this and that thing to Caesar?'* He keeps suggesting to us one thing after another to give to Caesar until one's whole life becomes Caesar's, and maybe only one percent remains for the Lord!

This is but one example of how the devil can deceive us into applying the verses in a way that suits our fallen and fleshly interests. We ought to know his devices and not be deceived by them.

Since the Word of God is one of the greatest resources by which we can resist the enemy and make him flee from us, the more we read it, memorise it, and use it in our prayers, the more it becomes a powerful tool in our mouth against the devil. As a result, when the devil brings his deceitful thoughts to our mind,[60] the Word of God protects us, giving us light and understanding; at the same time, it itself is a direct weapon against the enemy.

When we memorise it, the verses will spontaneously come to our minds when the devil attacks us. As we repeat the verses and proclaim them, the temptation that was distressing our minds and filling us with frustration and darkness disappears. Light comes to our minds, peace fills our souls, wounds are healed, confusion is dispelled and replaced with clarity, and our whole being is filled with peace and light.

---

59 Matthew 22:21

60 Deceit usually attacks the mind. The mind is one of the most common battlefields of the enemy, and deceit is one of the most common methods used by the devil (2 Corinthians 2:11).

The Book of Psalms is an important book of Scripture that the Church Fathers used as a tool in resisting the devil.[61] The Psalms have a special work and are effective because they are prayers that the Holy Spirit gave to the Psalmists David, Asaph, Korah, and others. He gave them these prayers during difficult circumstances which represent the confrontations between man and the powers of darkness. Therefore, the Psalms are the inspiration of the Holy Spirit to the tempted humanity, and hence are a direct tool against the devil.

When the Holy Spirit gives a Psalm to a person during times of difficulties and tribulations, this means that He gives him a spiritual tool to use against the devil and the powers of darkness.

3. Spiritual Weapons

Ephesians 6:10–18 outlines the main or general spiritual weapons, which are the girdle of truth, the breastplate of righteousness, the preparation of the gospel of peace, the shield of faith, the helmet of salvation, the sword of the Spirit, and praying always in the Spirit. There are also other references in various books of Scripture, such as the Book of Isaiah, that mention specific spiritual weapons that are of special importance. We will not go into this in detail as the aim here is to only give a brief overview.

To sum up:

There are three main principles and three main resources to overcome the devil.

---

61 1 Samuel 16:23

The three main principles are:

1. There is an unseen tempter, the devil, behind the visible temptations that we face. According to the rules of God's Kingdom, God never allows an evil power greater than us to confront us.
2. Therefore, we are able to be victorious in any confrontation. Scripture tells us that if we resist the enemy, he will flee from us.
3. However, we can be defeated in one of two cases: if we do not know (lack of knowledge) or if we know but do not obey (lack of faithfulness).

The three main resources are:

1. The Power of Redemption

This includes various resources or tools. We tend to focus on one and forget the others. However, if we know these resources in their broadness and richness, we will easily overcome the devil.

These tools are:

- The Blood of Jesus: *'They overcame him by the blood of the Lamb'* (Revelation 12:11).
- The Cross: *'Having disarmed principalities and powers, He made a public spectacle of them, triumphing over them in it'* (Colossians 2:15).
- The Resurrection: The proclamation of the victory
- The Ascension: When Christ ascended, He lifted us up with Him and seated us in Him above all ranks; thus, the devil is under our feet.
- The Holy Spirit: When the enemy comes like a flood, the breath of the Lord drives him away.

These resources have a faith aspect and a mystical aspect because the person is not only a spirit, but a spirit in a body. The Church calendar highlights the mystical aspect, including the season of the Cross and the seasons of the Resurrection, Ascension, and Pentecost. All these matters address the visible aspect in order to nourish the faith that is derived from the Word of God, so that our faith may be built and established.

Faith is a spiritual energy. It is built up and then used up. It is then built up again and used up again, and so on. Every time the enemy confronts us, we face him with this power of faith. In the battle, we lose some of this faith, and thus, we need to build it up again. Understanding what the Word of God says about redemption in all its aspects builds up our faith. Also, partaking in the mystical aspect through the Church services ignites our faith. Faith continues to be built and ignited, and then it is used in the battles, and then rebuilt, and so on and so forth. Notice that faith is not only built, but also ought to be ignited, which means that it is ready to be used. At the same time, it is not just used up and hence runs out, but it can also be rebuilt again and again.

2. The Power of the Word of God

The Book of Psalms holds a special place as a powerful tool against the enemy because it was given by the Holy Spirit to people who were going through temptations and confrontations with the devil.

3. The Power of Spiritual Weapons

The most important list of spiritual weapons is mentioned in Ephesians 6. Yet, there are other weapons mentioned in other books of Scripture, including the Book of Isaiah.[62]

---

62 Isaiah 59:17

Made in the USA
Coppell, TX
16 May 2026

77318667R00090